Revolution in the U.S. Information Infrastructure

National Academy of Engineering

NATIONAL ACADEMY PRESS
Washington, D.C. 1995

NATIONAL ACADEMY PRESS • 2101 Constitution Ave., NW • Washington, DC 20418

NOTICE: The National Academy of Engineering was established in 1964, under the charter of the National Academy of Sciences, as a parallel organization of outstanding engineers. It is autonomous in its administration and in the selection of its members, sharing with the National Academy of Sciences the responsibility for advising the federal government. The National Academy of Engineering also sponsors engineering programs aimed at meeting national needs, encourages education and research, and recognizes the superior achievement of engineers. Dr. Robert M. White is president of the National Academy of Engineering.

This publication has been reviewed by a group other than the authors according to procedures approved by a National Academy of Engineering report review process. The interpretations and conclusions expressed in this volume are those of the authors and are not presented as the views of the council, officers, or staff of the National Academy of Engineering.

Library of Congress Catalog Card Number 95-69120
International Standard Book Number 0-309-05287-4

Copyright 1995 by the National Academy of Sciences. All rights reserved.

Printed in the United States of America

Preface

Although terms like "national information infrastructure" and "information superhighway" have only recently become part of the vernacular, societies have always had information infrastructures. From mail carried by ship and Pony Express, to the telegraph, telephone and wireless, we have developed means and technologies that permit communication with others who are far from us. What is so dramatically different about today's information infrastructure, however, is its power and reach. Digital technology, optical transmission of information, and the continuing surge in the microchip's data-processing capability have spawned a spreading communications network throughout the world. These technological developments offer untold opportunities in fields as diverse as entertainment and industrial management. The public and private sectors are investing substantial sums to develop and implement the hard and soft infrastructure necessary to realize the promise of these advances.

Because of the complexity of the myriad undertakings now under way, and because the general public understands little of their implications, the National Academy of Engineering (NAE) decided to focus its 1994 Annual Meeting Technical Session on the revolution in the information infrastructure. The intent of the meeting, held October 6, 1994, in Washington, D.C., was to obtain the views of a diverse set of speakers whose current activities and future plans cover a broad range of approaches to the subject. The symposium addressed three broad questions:

- What technical and economic factors will determine the standards of and marketplace demand for products and services?
- What roles are government and private investment, demonstration projects, and regulation and regulatory reform likely to play in the development of the infrastructure during the next decade?
- What are the problems and promises for people's lives and organizations' work as video and data communications approach and surpass the interactivity of telephones?

As is reflected in the papers in this volume, the technological and market forces that are driving changes in the information infrastructure are fairly easy to identify. As is also evident in the papers, given the rapid evolution and growth in the infrastructure, there is a great diversity of opinion about how this future will come about. There is, however, agreement that rich technological capabilities and abundant market potentials will enhance the national information infrastructure and will lead ultimately, in a process already begun, to the realization of a global information infrastructure.

In addition to the authors, I would like to thank William R. Wulf for his illuminating and insightful closing remarks at the symposium. Other individuals who should be noted for their work, either in organizing the symposium or in getting this volume ready for publication, are Gerald Dinneen, Bruce Guile, Janet Hunziker, Greg Pearson, Vivienne Chin, Maribeth Keitz, and Mary Lee.

ROBERT M. WHITE
President
National Academy of Engineering

Contents

The Evolution of Information Infrastructures:
   The Competitive Search for Solutions   1
John S. Mayo

The Role of Government in the Evolution of the Internet   13
Robert E. Kahn

The Promise of the National Information Infrastructure   25
Robert W. Stearns

Satellite Communications in the Global Information
   Infrastructure   39
Steven D. Dorfman

Current Trends and Likely Futures in Wireless Systems   53
John E. Major

Antitrust Enforcement and the Telecommunications
   Revolution: Friends, Not Enemies   63
Robert E. Litan

Revolution in the U.S. Information Infrastructure

The Evolution of Information Infrastructures: The Competitive Search for Solutions

JOHN S. MAYO

While reflecting on what might be said about the "search for solutions" noted in the title of this paper, I recalled the story of the young executive who was about to leave the office at 6:00 p.m., when he found the boss standing with a piece of paper in front of the shredder.

"This is very important, and my secretary has left," said the boss. "Can you make this thing work?"

"Certainly, sir," said the young executive. He turned on the machine, inserted the paper, and pressed the start button.

"Excellent, excellent!" said the boss as his paper disappeared inside the machine, "I just need the one copy."

The message of this story is that a solution that has worked well in the past might be totally wrong for the problem at hand. This message also applies to the search for information infrastructure solutions.

With this in mind, I plan first to examine the driving forces that are propelling the emerging multimedia revolution and the evolution of information infrastructures. Then, I will discuss where these forces are taking us: to the National Information Infrastructure (NII) and, ultimately, to the Global Information Infrastructure (GII). Finally, I will briefly examine the consequences of this powerful and pervasive technological change on those involved in research and development.

FORCES DRIVING CHANGES IN THE INFORMATION INFRASTRUCTURE

It is no secret that information technology is the driving force and the key enabler of the emerging multimedia revolution and the evolution of the NII, as well as a host of other advances that together are changing the way we live, work, play, travel, and communicate. We have seen technological capability double every year in certain fields, such as computing and photonics, and double every 18 months in microelectronics. Even software, once a "bottleneck" technology, is beginning to advance rapidly in major areas like telecommunications, thanks to object-oriented programming and reuse of previously developed software modules.

Microelectronics

In microelectronics, we have witnessed the exponential growth of the familiar Moore Curve as the number of components per chip moves steadily toward known physical limits. In the early part of the next century, familiar "bulk effect" solid-state devices may mature with transistors that measure about 400 atoms by 400 atoms each— the smallest such transistor likely to operate reliably at room temperature. The new frontier then will not involve making the devices smaller, but in creatively and economically using the vast increase in complexity and power made possible by this remarkable technology.

The amazing progress of microelectronics represents a microcosm of the broad thrust of information technology and the other key driving forces made possible by information technology—all the most vital forces that are leading to the multimedia revolution and the evolution of the NII. Let me examine the progress and impact of these related forces.

After the invention of the integrated circuit, every time the complexity of silicon chips increased by a factor of a thousand, something had to be re-engineered. The first re-engineering that was done, as we headed toward that first thousandfold increase, was to change all of our design processes, which had been based on discrete components.

When we reached 1,000 components per chip, we used the new digital circuitry to re-engineer our products from analog to digital, as did many other industries. Let me stress that this early progress toward digital products, enabled by microelectronics and software, has brought about the digitalization of most systems and services domestically and, more and more, internationally. Digitalization is a powerful force driving us toward multimedia communications and the NII.

About a decade ago, it became possible to make chips approaching 1 million components, and this brought us powerful microcomputers, along with all the peripherals related to microcomputers and the necessary software systems. This led, in turn, to an explosion of advanced telecommunications services that forced AT&T to re-engineer itself from a company that provided largely voice and data-on-voice telecommunications services to one focused on universal information services, or the provision of voice, data, and images anywhere, anytime, with convenience and economy. Providing advanced services on an increasingly intelligent global network was the beginning of multimedia communications, which has now become the revolution of the 1990s and beyond.

We are currently experiencing another thousandfold increase in components per chip. Re-engineering has now extended beyond our company and is leading to the merging of communications, computers, consumer electronics, and entertainment. The convergence of these four industries is being accomplished through joint projects, joint ventures, mergers, acquisitions, and some start-up companies. This industrial re-engineering appears to be the next-to-last stage of the information revolution brought on by the invention of the transistor.

The last stage, and one that may go on forever, is the re-engineering of society—of how we live, work, play, travel, and communicate. Education will change with distance learning and home schooling; virtual offices and working at home will transform our work lives; routine tasks such as visiting and shopping more and more will be done from home. Let me add, however, that many of these changes will be generational; social change, as well as technology, is needed to make them happen.

Speech Processing

The trend toward increasingly powerful silicon chips is enabling exponential increases in the processing power of fixed-point digital signal processors. This trend makes it possible to use much less processing power to process a specific speech-recognition or speech-synthesis algorithm. Today, for example, a single chip can recognize a 100-word vocabulary, a function that would have required 20 to 30 chips 5 years ago.

Based on these advances, we can project that speaker-independent automatic speech recognition and synthesis will become commonplace. These technologies will mature in a variety of service capabilities based on the ability of intelligent machines to talk and listen much as people do. In addition, speech in one language will be automatically translated into a second language, which might then be synthesized with the voice characteristics of the original speaker. Virtually unrestricted recognition vocabulary will permit natural language interaction—with humans, machines, and databases.

Automatic speech recognition is vital to the multimedia revolution not because it replaces human operators, but because it is a powerful technology for making multimedia systems easy to use. Ease of use is an imperative for broad marketplace success.

Image Processing

The emerging technology of image processing is related in many respects to speech processing and is another driving force toward multimedia communications and the evolution of our information infrastructure. The same key information technologies that are enabling progress in speech processing are also fueling rapid progress in image processing, especially in the important areas of image and video compression.

Consider video compression. At the network capacity of two Integrated Services Digital Network (ISDN) Basic Rate Interface channels, or 128 kilobits per second, we can have video that is compressed using the so-called p X 64 international standard for videotelephony, for person-to-person communications. This standard was designed for sending videotelephony over phone lines in multiples of 64 kilobits per second. At this capacity, we have the ISDN videophone, which is likely to be a highly attractive product as long as copper wires make up the local telephone plant. At the network capacity of 1.5 megabits per second, we can have high-quality desktop video compressed with the maximum level of the p X 64 standard. This network capacity can support National Television System Committee (NTSC) color television with VHS quality, using the Moving Picture Experts Group (MPEG) standards, which are designed for capturing moving images on CD-ROM and for storing and transmitting movies and broadcast television. However, with available compression technology, a capacity of 1.5 megabits per second would not deliver broadcast quality for scenes with rapid motion and detail.

The network capacity of 45 megabits per second will readily support high-definition TV (HDTV) compressed to about 20 megabits per second, using variations of the MPEG-2 coding algorithm. That is a considerable reduction (about 50:1 compression) from the roughly 1 billion bits per second required for uncompressed HDTV. That same network capacity will also support near studio-quality video (HDTV or NTSC) that has been compressed by using variations of the identical coding algorithm.

Common Standards

Another force driving the progress of multimedia communications and the evolution of the information infrastructure is the worldwide push toward common standards that will encourage global networking. Photonic transmission facilities, for example, will be based on the evolving international standard called SDH, for Synchronous Digital Hierarchy. Because SDH defines standard network interfaces, service providers and end users will be able to use equipment from many different vendors without worrying about compatibility. SDH will provide efficient transport of broadband services and will simplify networks. Similar standards in domestic networks will allow digital communications into the workplace and home, and they will make possible services dependent on high rates of data transmission.

Broadband Integrated Services Digital Network (B-ISDN) is a new digital format as well as an international standard that supports multiple services, such as voice, data, and new video services, using fiber-optic transmission facilities. B-ISDN is currently defined at interface rates of 155 megabits per second and 622 megabits per second. Based on the fast-packet technology of asynchronous transfer mode (ATM), B-ISDN could herald an exciting new era in global communications networking, as equipment vendors and service providers adopt compatible standards to provide sophisticated high-bandwidth services.

Market Demand

The demands of the marketplace, more than technology, set the pace for the multimedia and infrastructure revolution. For the greater part of this century, the customer willingly accepted whatever technological capabilities we were able to achieve. Thus, the telecommunications industry was supplier driven, and the suppliers managed the evolution of the industry and the NII. However, the technology became so rich that it made possible many more products and services than the user could accept or was willing to pay for. That marked the transition from a supplier-driven industry to today's customer-driven industry—from supplier push to marketplace pull.

Competition

The global transfer and assimilation of information technology, along with political and regulatory forces, such as the move to privatize telecommunications around the world, are leading to strong international competition in providing communications products and services. Such pervasive competition is another powerful force driving the evolution of both multimedia communications and information infrastructures. The public policy challenge is to provide a framework in which that evolution may occur.

THE MULTIMEDIA REVOLUTION

Let us look a bit deeper into these subjects, starting with the multimedia revolution. After all, the pursuit of multimedia is creating social pressures on the NII and the information superhighways. So, what is "multimedia"? A reasonable working definition is that the term multimedia refers to information that combines more than one medium, including speech, music, text, data, graphics, fax, image, video, and animation. At AT&T, we tend to focus on multimedia products and services that are networked, or connected over a communications and information network. Examples of this range from videotelephony and videoconferencing; to real-time video on demand, interactive video, and multimedia messaging; to remote collaborative work, interactive information services such as electronic shopping, and multimedia education and training. Eventually, we will have virtual reality, which will enable people to experience a place or an event indirectly and remotely—and do so in all dimensions.

We are excited about multimedia because public switched networks, or information infrastructures, can currently accommodate a wide array of networked multimedia communications. Given the directions in which those networks are evolving, they will be able to handle an increasingly vast range of such communications. Moreover, a potentially enormous market is out there for multimedia hardware and supporting software. Although estimates differ widely, the most commonly quoted projection for the total worldwide market for multimedia products and services is roughly $100 billion by the year 2000.

AT&T is playing a major part in facilitating the emerging multimedia revolution: We provide services, network products to local service providers, and products to end users. These are familiar roles for AT&T, so let me briefly describe another perhaps less well known aspect of the multimedia revolution that we are studying. That role is as the host for a wide variety of digital content and multimedia applications developed by others. Hosting is a function that connects end users to the content they seek. Customers will gain easy and timely access to personal communications, transactions, information services, and entertainment via wired and wireless connections to telephones, handheld devices, computers, and, eventually, television sets. Sources for this digital content will range from publishers and large movie studios to small software houses.

Global standards and open critical interfaces are vital to this complex hosting function. The entertainment industry, for example, must have software systems that are compatible with those of the hosting industry. These software systems must, in turn, be compatible with those of the communications and information-networking industry, which must be compatible with customer premises equipment and systems.

In the age of multimedia communications, consumers who are geographically separated from each other will do more than just play games together over networks. According to the AT&T vision, people will increasingly seek new relationships based on "telepresence"—a new type of community and social experience independent of geography. This potential for interactive networks is quite unlike what will result from the 500 preprogrammed cable TV channels proposed for the United States. The beauty of interactive networks is that consumers will have the freedom to choose any subject or service from the intelligent terminals in their homes. And they will be able to network clusters of friends or associates to enjoy such services as a group.

Although I have focused heavily on the impact that multimedia will have on the consumer, networked multimedia communications will dramatically change the nature of work and will therefore have a broad effect on business. Videoconferencing, for example, can enhance productivity, save time, and reduce travel. Moreover, current developments in multimedia telephony are making realistic the possibility of remote collaboration. In a few years, a person could be working in real time with colleagues in New York, Washington, Hong Kong, Paris, and Sydney. They could, for example, accomplish the task of producing printed materials, presentation slides, and a videotape introducing a new product line.

EVOLUTION OF THE NII

The quest for multimedia is driving social issues that relate to the NII and the information superhighway. The NII might be viewed as the superhighway plus all the terminals and databases connected to it.

What is AT&T's vision of the NII? It is to bring people together, giving them easy access to each other and to the information and services they want and need, any time, anywhere. In AT&T's view, the NII is a seamless web of communications and information networks, computers, databases, and consumer electronics, which will put huge quantities of information at the fingertips of a variety of users. Quite simply, we see the communications component of the NII as a vast interoperable network of local, long-distance, and global networks; wireless; broadcast and cable; and satellites. In addition, the NII encompasses the Internet as well as the test beds associated with the High-Performance Computing Initiative, such as the

Blanca test bed with which AT&T is affiliated. However, the NII is not a uniform end-to-end network developed and operated by government or any one company. It is the totality of networks in our nation, interconnected domestically and internationally.

These networks consist of a wide variety of technologies that provide a complete range of features and transport speeds. In the United States, competitive backbone information superhighways of optical fibers are already in place and expanding rapidly. However, access to the backbone is still largely via copper wire pairs, especially for homes, schools, and small businesses. Many consumers and small firms will be able to get substantial value from the NII using recent technological advances, such as ISDN. Genuine and effective competition in the local exchange is a long-term possibility and is the key to advancing the deployment of needed digital and higher-bandwidth access services. We also believe that the coaxial cables of the CATV networks can become important elements of the nation's broadband superhighways.

One key to making this network of networks a true global information superhighway for multimedia and other communications is a system of open, user-friendly interfaces and global standards. Such a system both promotes maximum interoperability and connectivity and supports a multivendor environment that allows maximum customer choice of equipment and services.

To ensure that people can use whatever NII capabilities they need when they need them, a range of bandwidth offerings should be made available.

Several policy issues are associated with the NII:

(1) The government should help provide the vision for the way the NII will evolve and operate. Private industry should build, own, and operate the NII under competitive conditions.

(2) The government should provide incentives and opportunities, such as tax credits for investment in equipment, R&D, or worker training, to encourage the private sector to invest in and deploy new information technology. The government should continue to focus its direct support on precompetitive projects or applications that demonstrate and test new NII technologies.

(3) In order to realize the broad benefits of the multimedia revolution and the NII, there must be full and fair competition in all

sectors of our communications and information industry, both domestically and internationally.

(4) Private industry must continue to play the lead role in working to define the interoperability standards of the NII. The government must continue to work with and represent industry in some international treaty organizations that develop standards. Jointly, we need to speed up the standards-setting process.

(5) Perhaps the broadest policy challenge is that of facilitating public acceptance of and comfort with the benefits of multimedia communications and the NII. This will require setting ground rules to protect electronically available intellectual property, creating a framework to ensure privacy and security of information, and establishing mechanisms to make these benefits available to the largest number of users. This last point is vital if we are to avoid having a nation of information "haves" and "have nots." The challenge, simply put, is to develop a new definition of universal service.

Fortunately, most of the key issues and challenges surrounding multimedia and the NII are already being addressed by cooperative government and private-sector efforts. Much more remains to be done. The ultimate resolution of these issues will require the support of all of us.

IMPACT ON R&D

At the beginning of this paper, I noted that a solution that has worked well in the past might be totally wrong for the problem at hand. This applies broadly to R&D and R&D environments. The forces behind the emerging multimedia revolution and the evolution of information infrastructures, along with the benefits associated with the information age, are also bringing about a new paradigm for R&D and a new R&D environment.

The traditional R&D approach of past decades was to use prototyping and redesign: to do, then learn, and then redo as often as necessary to produce a good product, and to do so through serial handoffs from one function to another. Today, that approach is not competitive because of the increasingly complex and rapid advances of information technology, multimedia communications, and information infrastructures. The marketplace demands more and cheaper products and services with ever-shorter delivery intervals. In addition, an increasing demand exists for the customization of products to ever-smaller buying units.

Thus, in contrast to the traditional R&D approach, we must pursue concurrent engineering, together with the important integration function of deciding and planning precisely what to do before we build anything. Instead of talking to the customer after we complete a project, we do so before starting, because the customer is really in control. The vital integration function, which helps ensure that the product or service works the first time, is becoming an ever-larger piece of the R&D effort.

Functionally structured R&D has yielded to customer-focused, multifunctional teams. This shift has helped generate a new R&D paradigm and a new R&D environment with very different processes and demands on people. Let me illustrate with the typical challenge of trying to pursue a number of R&D projects at once. Within today's lean, cost-effective R&D organizations, there are usually many more projects than there are expert staff. Therefore, dedicating these experts to specific projects would result in poor overall project performance. Instead, support systems must facilitate the training and sharing of expertise, most often through well-orchestrated multifunctional teams and new techniques for learning, including a strong focus on intergroup learning.

Another key element of the new R&D paradigm and its associated environment is a focus on reusable assets, such as previously designed and tested software modules and hardware platforms. Reusable assets facilitate the creation of products and services from higher-level elements. They enable organizations to share key skills across projects and create world-class experts, while also developing rapid and cost-effective solutions, customizations, and competitive advantage. Reusable assets are the most powerful mechanism we have today for improving R&D productivity. Proper use of such assets can make possible perhaps as much as a tenfold improvement in design productivity. The reusable-asset concept also extends to families of reusable processes, which unify architectures and facilitate efficient realization of products and services.

Structuring R&D around reusable assets produces an environment in which research is more important than ever. A major part of doing good research is finding good problems on which to work.

Bell Labs has never had to look far; every day we face many real problems for which we do not have good solutions. Moreover, research results are themselves reusable assets; they help reduce the development effort and shorten the development interval. The new R&D approach also yields lower costs and higher quality.

The new R&D paradigm and R&D environment cannot by themselves fulfill the demands of the new marketplace paradigm of growth through new corporate structures, new customers, and new competitors. R&D, however, must play the important role of identifying the new opportunities and parameters that a corporation must pursue with its total resources.

SUMMARY

Rich information technology, the worldwide push toward global standards, ever-increasing customer demands, and growing international competition are key forces behind the emerging multimedia revolution and the evolution of national information infrastructures. The growth of multimedia communications and the further competitive evolution of our National Information Infrastructure, as well as the Global Information Infrastructure, raise some difficult issues and challenges, but these advances promise a broad range of information-age benefits to virtually every citizen of our nation.

Already, we find that yesterday's R&D solutions are no longer adequate for the revolution at hand. A new R&D paradigm for a new R&D environment is developing rapidly. And each and every one of us, especially those in R&D, must understand and assimilate this new paradigm. We must ensure that it both serves society well and creates an environment in which the best minds of the world seek careers in science and engineering. Long-term progress depends on it, and it can be done.

The Role of Government in the Evolution of the Internet

ROBERT E. KAHN

This paper discusses the role of government in the continuing evolution of the Internet. From its origins as a U.S. government research project, the Internet has grown to become a major component of network infrastructure, linking millions of machines and tens of millions of users around the world. Although many nations are now involved with the Internet in one way or another, this paper focuses on the primary role the U.S. government has played in the Internet's evolution and discusses the role that governments around the world may have to play as it continues to develop.

Very little of the current Internet is owned, operated, or even controlled by governmental bodies. The Internet indirectly receives government support through federally funded academic facilities that provide some network-related services. Increasingly, however, the provision of Internet communication services, regardless of use, is being handled by commercial firms on a profit-making basis.

This situation raises the question of the proper long-term role for government in the continued evolution of the Internet. Is the Internet now in a form where government involvement should cease entirely, leaving private-sector interests to determine its future? Or, does

---

A version of this paper appeared in the August 1994 issue of *Communications of the ACM*.

government still have an important role to play? This paper concludes that government can still make a series of important contributions. Indeed, there are a few areas in which government involvement will be vital to the long-term well-being of the Internet.

ORIGINS OF THE INTERNET

The Internet originated in the early 1970s as part of an Advanced Research Projects Agency (ARPA) research project on "internetworking." At that time, ARPA demonstrated the viability of packet switching for computer-to-computer communication in its flagship network, the ARPANET, which linked several dozen sites and perhaps twice that number of computers into a national network for computer science research. Extensions of the packet-switching concept to satellite networks and to ground-based mobile radio networks were also under development by ARPA, and segments of industry (notably not the traditional telecommunications sector) were showing great interest in providing commercial packet network services. It seemed likely that at least three or four distinct computer networks would exist by the mid-1970s and that the ability to communicate among these networks would be highly desirable if not essential.

In a well-known joint effort that took place around 1973, Robert Kahn, then at ARPA, and Vinton Cerf, then at Stanford, collaborated on the design of an internetwork architecture that would allow packet networks of different kinds to interconnect and machines to communicate across the set of interconnected networks. The internetwork architecture was based on a protocol that came to be known as TCP/IP. The period from 1974 to 1978 saw four successively refined versions of the protocol implemented and tested by ARPA research contractors in academia and industry, with version number four eventually becoming standardized. The TCP/IP protocol was used initially to connect the ARPANET, based on 50 kilobits per second (kbps) terrestrial lines; the Packet Radio Net (PRNET), based on dual rate 400/100 kbps spread spectrum radios; and the Packet Satellite Net (SATNET), based on a 64 kbps shared channel on Intelsat IV. The initial satellite Earth stations were in the United States and the United Kingdom, but subsequently additional Earth stations were activated in Norway, Germany, and Italy. Several experimental PRNETs were connected, including one in the San Francisco Bay area. At the time, no personal computers, workstations, or local area networks were available commercially, and the machines involved were mainly large-scale scientific time-sharing systems. Remote access to time-sharing systems was made available by terminal access servers.

The technical tasks involved in constructing this initial ARPA Internet revolved mainly around the configuration of "gateways," now known as routers, to connect different networks, as well as the development of TCP/IP software in the computers. These were both engineering-intensive tasks that took considerable expertise to accomplish. By the mid-1980s, industry began offering commercial gateways and routers and started to make available TCP/IP software for some workstations, minicomputers, and mainframes. Before this, these capabilities were unavailable; they had to be handcrafted by the engineers at each site.

In 1979, ARPA established a small Internet Configuration Control Board (ICCB), most of whose members belonged to the research community, to help with this process and to work with ARPA in evolving the Internet design. The establishment of the ICCB was important because it brought a wider segment of the research community into the Internet decision-making process, which until then had been the almost-exclusive bailiwick of ARPA. Initially, the ICCB was chaired by a representative of ARPA and met several times a year. As interest in the ARPA Internet grew, so did interest in the work of the ICCB.

During this early period, the U.S. government, mainly ARPA, funded research and development work on networks and supported the various networks in the ARPA Internet by leasing and buying components and contracting out the system's day-to-day operational management. The government also maintained responsibility for overall policy. In the mid- to late 1970s, experimental local area networks and experimental workstations, which had been developed in the research community, were connected to the Internet according to the level of engineering expertise at each site. In the early 1980s, Internet-compatible commercial workstations and local area networks became available, significantly easing the task of getting connected to the Internet.

The U.S. government also awarded contracts for the support of various aspects of Internet infrastructure, including the maintenance of lists of hosts and their addresses on the network. Other government-funded groups monitored and maintained the key gateways between the Internet networks in addition to supporting the networks themselves. In 1980, the U.S. Department of Defense (DOD) adopted the TCP/IP protocol as a standard and began to use it. By the early 1980s, it was clear that the internetwork architecture that ARPA had created was a viable technology for wider use in defense.

EMERGENCE OF THE OPERATIONAL INTERNET

The DOD had become convinced that if its use of networking were to grow, it needed to split the ARPA Internet (called ARPANET) in two. One of the resulting networks, to be known as MILNET, would be used for military purposes and mainly link military sites in the United States. The remaining portion of the network would continue to bear the name ARPANET and still be used for research purposes. Since both would use the TCP/IP protocol, computers on the MILNET would still be able to talk to computers on the new ARPANET, but the MILNET network nodes would be located at protected sites. If problems developed on the ARPANET, the MILNET could be disconnected quickly from it by unplugging the small number of gateways that connected them. In fact, these gateways were designed to limit the interactions between the two networks to the exchange of electronic mail, a further safety feature.

By the early 1980s, the ARPA Internet was known simply as the Internet, and the number of connections to it continued to grow. Recognizing the importance of networking to the larger computer science community, the National Science Foundation (NSF) began supporting CSNET, which connected a select group of computer science researchers to the emerging Internet. This allowed new research sites to be placed on the ARPANET at NSF's expense, and it allowed other new research sites to be connected via a commercial network, TELENET, which would be gatewayed to the ARPANET. CSNET also provided the capacity to support dial-up e-mail connections. In addition, access to the ARPANET was informally extended to researchers at numerous sites, thus helping to further spread the networking technology within the scientific community. Also during this period, other federal agencies with computer-oriented research programs, notably the Department of Energy (DOE) and the National

Aeronautics and Space Administration (NASA), created their own "community networks."

The TCP/IP protocol adopted by DOD a few years earlier was only one of many such standards. Although it was the only one that dealt explicitly with internetworking of packet networks, its use was not yet mandated on the ARPANET. However, on January 1, 1983, TCP/IP became the standard for the ARPANET, replacing the older host protocol known as NCP. This step was in preparation for the ARPANET-MILNET split, which was to occur about a year later. Mandating the use of TCP/IP on the ARPANET encouraged the addition of local area networks and also accelerated the growth in numbers of users and networks. At the same time, it led to a rethinking of the process that ARPA was using to manage the evolution of the network.

In 1983, ARPA replaced the ICCB with the Internet Activities Board (IAB). The IAB was constituted similarly to the old ICCB, but the many issues of network evolution were delegated to 10 task forces chartered by and reporting to the IAB. The IAB was charged with assisting ARPA to meet its Internet-related R&D objectives; the chair of the IAB was selected from the research community supported by ARPA. ARPA also began to delegate to the IAB the responsibility for conducting the standards-setting process.

Following the CSNET effort, NSF and ARPA worked together to expand the number of users on the ARPANET, but they were constrained by the limitations that DOD placed on the use of the network. By the mid-1980s, however, network connectivity had become sufficiently central to the workings of the computer science community that NSF became interested in broadening the use of networking to other scientific disciplines. The NSF supercomputer centers program represented a major stimulus to broader use of networks by providing limited access to the centers via the ARPANET. At about the same time, ARPA decided to phase out its network research program, only to reconsider this decision about a year later when the seeds for the subsequent high-performance computer initiative were planted by the Reagan administration and then-Sen. Albert Gore (D-Tenn.). In this period, NSF formulated a strategy to assume responsibility for the areas of leadership that ARPA had formerly held and planned to field an advanced network called NSFNET. NSFNET was to join the NSF supercomputer centers with very high speed links, then 1.5 megabits per second (mbps), and to provide members of the U.S. academic community access to the NSF supercomputer centers and to one another.[1]

Under a cooperative agreement between NSF and Merit, Inc., the NSFNET backbone was put into operation in 1988 and, because of its higher speed, soon replaced the ARPANET as the backbone of choice. In 1990, ARPA decommissioned the last node of the ARPANET. It was replaced by the NSFNET backbone and a series of regional networks most of which were funded by or at least started with funds from the U.S. government and were expected to become self-supporting soon thereafter. The NSF effort greatly expanded the involvement of many other groups in providing as well as using network services. This expansion followed as a direct result of the planning for the High Performance Computing Initiative (HPCI), which was being formed at the highest levels of government. DOD still retained the responsibility for control of the Internet name and address space, although it continued to contract out the operational aspects of the system.

The DOE and NASA both rely heavily on networking capability to support their missions. In the early 1980s, they built High Energy Physics Net (HEPNET) and Space Physics Analysis Net (SPAN), both based on Digital Equipment Corporation's DECNET protocols. Later, DOE and NASA developed the Energy Sciences Net (ESNET) and the NASA Science Internet (NSI), respectively; these networks supported both TCP/IP and DECNET services. These initiatives were early influences on the development of the multiprotocol networking technology that was subsequently adopted in the Internet.

International networking activity was also expanding in the early and mid-1980s. Starting with a number of networks based on the X.25 standard as well as international links to ARPANET, DECNET, and SPAN, the networks began to incorporate open internetworking protocols. Initially, Open Systems Interconnection (OSI) protocols were used most frequently. Later, the same forces that drove the United States to use TCP/IP—availability in commercial workstations and local area networks—caused the use of TCP/IP to grow internationally.

---

[1] For a brief period in the mid-1980s, there was a small initial NSFNET that linked the supercomputer centers with 64 kbps lines.

The number of task forces under the IAB continued to grow, and in 1989, the IAB consolidated them into two groups: the Internet Engineering Task Force (IETF) and the Internet Research Task Force (IRTF). The IETF, which had been formed as one of the original 10 IAB Task Forces, was given responsibility for near-term Internet developments and for generating options for the IAB to consider as Internet standards. The IRTF remained much smaller than the IETF and focused more on longer-range research issues. The IAB structure, with its task-force mechanism, opened up the possibility of getting broader involvement from the private sector without the need for government to pay directly for their participation. The federal role continued to be limited to oversight control of the Internet name and address space, the support of IETF meetings, and sponsorship of many of the research participants. By the end of the 1980s, IETF began charging a nominal attendance fee to cover the costs of its meetings.

The opening of the Internet to commercial usage was a significant development in the late 1980s. As a first step, commercial e-mail providers were allowed to use the NSFNET backbone to communicate with authorized users of the NSFNET and other federal research networks. Regional networks, initially established to serve the academic community, had in their efforts to become self-sufficient taken on nonacademic customers as an additional revenue source. NSF's Acceptable Use Policy, which restricted backbone usage to traffic within and for the support of the academic community, together with the growing number of nonacademic Internet users, led to the formation of two privately funded and competing Internet carriers, both spin-offs of U.S. government programs. They were UUNET Technologies, a product of a DOD-funded seismic research facility, and Performance Systems International (PSI), which was formed by a subset of the officers and directors of NYSERNET, the NSF-sponsored regional network in New York and the lower New England states.

Beginning in 1990, Internet use was growing by more than 10 percent a month. This expansion was fueled significantly by the enormous growth on the NSFNET and included a major commercial and international component. NSF helped to stimulate this growth by funding both incremental and fundamental improvements in Internet routing technology as well as by encouraging the widespread distribution of network software from its supercomputer centers. Interconnections between commercial and other networks are arranged in a variety of ways, including through the use of the Commercial Internet Exchange (CIX), which was established, in part, to facilitate packet exchanges among commercial service providers.

Recently, the NSF decided that additional funding for the NSFNET backbone no longer was required. The agency embarked on a plan to make the NSF regional networks self supporting over a period of several years. To assure the scientific research community of continued network access, NSF made competitively chosen awards to several parties to provide network access points (NAPs) in four cities. NSF also selected MCI to provide a very high speed backbone service, initially at 155 mbps, linking the NAPs and several other sites, and a routing arbiter to oversee certain aspects of traffic allocation in this new architecture.

The Internet Society was formed in 1992 by the private sector to help promote the evolution of the Internet, including maintenance of the Internet standards process. In 1992, the IAB was reconstituted as the Internet Architecture Board, which became part of the Internet Society. It delegated its decision-making responsibility on Internet standards to the leadership of the IETF, known as the Internet Engineering Steering Group (IESG). While not a part of the Internet Society, the IETF produces technical specifications as possible candidates for future protocols. The Internet Society now maintains the Internet Standards Process, and the work of the IETF is carried out under its auspices.

ISSUES FOR CONSIDERATION

As the Internet continues to grow, the role of the research community in developing and evolving standards needs to be addressed. When the financial implications of decisions about Internet standards were relatively small, the current standards process proved entirely satisfactory. As the financial impact of such decisions becomes increasingly significant, the nature of the standards-setting process will continue to change to allow more direct industrial involvement. How this will ultimately play out is unclear. However, the vitality of the current process derives from the broad involvement of the many communities that have a stake in the Internet. Unlike typical top-down standards-setting operations that implement decisions formed by consensus, the Internet process works essentially in reverse through a kind of grass-roots mechanism. Candidates for Internet standards ordinarily result from actual implementation and widespread experimentation within the IETF. The most promising of these candidates are selected for placement on the Internet standards track. No better process has yet emerged that is as dynamic and allows as much direct involvement by industry.

Further, with the widespread internationalization of the Internet, scores of countries now have fundamental interests in its evolution. Within the United States, the Internet is seen in many quarters as the starting point for the National Information Infrastructure (NII). Around the world, there is growing recognition that the set of NIIs (assuming each country commits to developing one) should be compatible with each other along some still-unknown dimensions. Who should take the lead in ensuring this compatibility? Is this a role for the private sector, for governments acting together, or for some combination of the two? There is clearly a role for government, at least to provide oversight, support, and guidance, if not to participate actively.

Apart from these issues is concern about the viability of any approach that has no individual or organization with overall responsibility for its evolution. It seems fair to say that many of the traditional Internet carriers would prefer that new capabilities be provided by them as a turnkey service. Industry surely has the capacity to provide many of the necessary capabilities, but history has shown the importance of government involvement. What guarantees that the same degree of vitality will be part of its future evolution if market forces alone determine what new capabilities are added to the Internet? Furthermore, the Internet offers the possibility of bypassing conventional service offerings by regulated carriers. This may both make it extremely difficult for the regulated carriers to compete effectively in certain areas and make it hard for government regulators to ignore the Internet.

Finally, the carriers can only go so far in providing Internet services. Ultimately, the communication pathways must enter the user's machine, pass through layers of software and end up in applications programs. The computer industry, along with the many vendors of computer-related equipment, must play a role in determining how this aspect of the Internet will evolve. The nature of technological innovation almost guarantees that many new technological options will continue to be generated from many different sources and make their appearance throughout the Internet. Thus, it appears that no single entity can possibly be in charge of the Internet. A key to the success of the Internet is to insure that the interested parties have a fair and equitable way of participating in its evolution, including participation in its also-evolving standards process. A proper role for governments would be to oversee this process to make sure that it remains fair and meets the wide spectrum of public needs.

An international infrastructure like the Internet will ultimately require countries to set policy on many of the details that are now taken for granted. For example, Internet names and addresses may take on additional legal meanings in the various countries as they rely on the Internet to a greater degree. Trademark of Internet names and addresses is only one aspect of concern. Contracts of all sorts may have Internet names and addresses embedded within them. How can the countries have confidence in the use of such names and addresses for legal purposes without necessarily assuming responsibility for the day-to-day operation of this aspect of the system? Computer viruses know no national boundaries. If a major "infection" should strike multiple countries, how will those countries work together to respond to such a situation? Finally, the ability to conduct network-based business between countries will require the resolution of many legal issues, including the formalization of legal contracts online and the ability to deal with associated customs and trade-related matters. At its core, the issue of online legal contracts seems to require the use of encryption technology, which has been perhaps the most closely held of all the network-oriented technologies. How can this kind of capability be made available in the international arena in ways that are acceptable to national authorities? More generally, how can issues like those described above, which are likely to arise in the future, be effectively discussed and resolved?

Various subsets of these kinds of problems have arisen in the context of other international public networks, including for telephones, and are thus neither unique nor entirely new. As the Internet continues to grow, many of the approaches developed for earlier technologies may apply to the Internet. Some combination of public- and private-sector involvement will probably be required to deal with these problems more generally.

Governments have a fundamental role to play in the funding of advanced research and development that can push forward the frontiers of technology and knowledge. Often, this will involve the development and use of pilot projects to test new ideas in the real world. It also seems clear that governments must provide the necessary oversight to insure that the standards-setting process is equitable. Governments must also take responsibility for helping to resolve problems that arise because of independent decisions made by multiple countries, for example in legal, security, or regulatory matters. In the case of U.S. infrastructure development, the government must provide leadership in many dimensions, including the removal of barriers where they inhibit progress; the insertion of legal, security, or regulatory mechanisms where the national interest so dictates; and the direct stimulation of public-interest sectors, for example in research, education, and certain network aspects of public health, safety, and universal access that require government assistance. Other nations also may find similar incentives for government involvement.

Two final observations seem appropriate. First, it will be essential to separate the process by which standards are selected for the Internet from the process by which the variety of possible options are generated. The current situation is almost ideal, since standards are selected by a process akin to ratification only after independent implementation has produced the viable options. This separation needs to be maintained.

Second, the most important use of the Internet, and indeed the NII, will be to allow individuals to communicate with each other and to rapidly access information. In many cases, this information will be the intellectual property of others. Every Internet user will also have the opportunity to become a potential provider of information services, thereby vastly increasing the amount of information available. How much of this information may be deemed valuable in a literary or business sense remains to be determined, but much of it may be important in other contexts. It is essential that we sensitize individuals to the value of intellectual property and the need to protect it. This will have the side benefit of encouraging others to develop and make available intellectual property of their own. A combination of ethics, technology, and law are needed to ensure the effective development of this important aspect of the Internet.

CONCLUSIONS

Over a span of some 20 years, the role of the U.S. government in the evolution of the Internet has changed. While the federal government took the lead in virtually every aspect of Internet in the early days, it currently plays a more limited role. The government is now a major funder of network R&D and provides significant oversight of the evolution of the Internet. It provides direct support or even control for several key aspects of the Internet's operation, such as the assignment of unique names and addresses and the assurance of adequate backbone capability, although it may decide to relinquish some of these responsibilities in the future. It continues to stimulate the development of Internet architecture in healthy new directions.

Although the role of the U.S. government in the Internet has been declining steadily for several years, particularly as private-sector interest in the Internet has increased, there is a major continuing set of roles and responsibilities for government to undertake, both in the United States and around the world. Governments must be involved in decisions about how different countries cooperate on various aspects of the Internet and its use, and they must continue to oversee the network's evolution, both nationally and internationally. Other national governments may, but need not, assume the leadership role that the U.S. government has traditionally played in the United States. Without substantial U.S. involvement however, it is doubtful whether the NII will become a reality. And without government involvement on an international scale, it is unlikely that a global information infrastructure will emerge or that the Internet will continue to evolve in a vital and dynamic way.

Taking a long view, network and computer technologies are still in their infancy, and many of their current uses reflect past practices carried out more effectively in new environments. The real challenge will be for the public and private sectors to work together to harness the still-untapped potential of new and increasingly powerful technologies in the network-based setting of the NII, and to nourish and incubate the powerful, even revolutionary, new ideas that are certain to surface in the future.

The Promise of the National Information Infrastructure

ROBERT W. STEARNS

There is a computer industry joke that is very relevant to a discussion of the National Information Infrastructure (NII). It explains why God was able to create the universe in 6 days: He did not have an installed base.

Creating the NII is certainly not as vast a task as creating the universe, although the concept does seem to have boundless potential. The joke came to mind because realizing this potential will require careful navigation through the baggage of old technologies and partisan and entrenched points of view in industry, government, and academia.

Underlying the sometimes overblown talk about the information superhighway is a widespread recognition that information technology has the potential to dramatically change many aspects of our lives. We also are recognizing that information systems have the potential to play a central role in reinvigorating many of the institutions of our society.

Over the last decade, information technology has been an essential tool for corporations. It has enabled the cost cutting, reorganization, and re-engineering that have helped re-establish the United States' global competitiveness and rejuvenated many U.S. companies. We are now discovering that this technology could have a similar effect on our noncorporate lives: It could change the ways we educate our children and ourselves, interact with government, manage our health, and entertain and socialize. At Compaq, we believe we play a central role in the development of the NII, particularly as the computer evolves from a device used principally for computation to one that is dominantly used for communication.

There are, of course, many different definitions of the NII, depending on one's business and/or political perspective. NII has been described variously as: a 500-channel interactive multimedia video/cable network; numerous "edutainment" multimedia products and services; the natural evolution of today's telephone system from one that is voice-oriented to one that supports voice, data, image, and video; an electronic marketplace for commercial and/or consumer products and services; a commercial version of the Internet; a public network for government information and services, medical information, and education; not a single network at all but a loose aggregate of many different networks and services with common or related access; a public-policy debate about social rights and access to information; a political battle in which the telecommunication and cable industries may attempt to reassert their monopolies in the name of universal service; and a government-funded initiative, created by the Clinton administration and modeled after the National Highway Project of the late 1950s and 1960s, which could easily turn into a new species of high-technology pork.

Whatever the technical description, five key issues dominate policy discussions:

Universal service. All Americans should have easy access to the NII, at least for some basic level of services yet to be defined.

Interoperability. Legacy and future platform devices such as computers and phones, software applications, and databases should be able to "talk" to each other easily via the highway.

Security, privacy, and protection of intellectual property. The content and nature of communications on the NII should be carefully protected from eavesdropping, misappropriation, or unauthorized use.

Private-sector versus public-sector model. Should the NII evolve in a basically unregulated environment that responds to free-market forces, or should the federal government fund and guide its development?

NII's link to the GII. Is the global information infrastructure truly a worldwide, unified system or the aggregate of individual service networks?

With these issues as context, I would like to review the recent history of the information industry and attempt to characterize the probable nature of the industry in the future. I will also explain why the PC may well play a central role and give some examples of technology use that exemplify the fundamental promise of the NII. Finally, I will outline the key challenges to realizing the full potential of the NII and identify some principles that should guide us as we move forward.

THE INFORMATION INDUSTRY

Underlying the information revolution has been the dramatic pace of innovation in semiconductor technologies, fiber optics, voice and data communications, and software. These innovations have enabled a shift from incompatible analog technologies to interoperable digital technologies and have brought about the convergence of computers, telecommunications, and media. The information user has received an unprecedented improvement in features and a sharp reduction in cost.

The industry structure that is emerging, although confusing, can be divided into three basic categories: platform providers, conduit providers, and content providers. Platform providers include vendors of the hardware and software building blocks of personal and corporate computing. Conduit providers establish the electronic highways through which the information flows. Content providers develop and commercialize the software applications, information, and entertainment that flow through the highways to and from the platforms.

These three categories of providers are inextricably linked. The computer will increasingly be an access, processing, and storage point on the network. The network will increasingly be designed and built with a higher and higher percentage of the intelligence lying outside the conduit in the devices connected to the network. The content providers will increasingly develop their products in multiple versions to be compatible with the multiple technologies that will be used to distribute these products.

It is no longer possible for any one provider, by itself, to move the development of the information infrastructure. Innovations to the platform, without a supporting network and content that people want, will not succeed. Equally useless are network developments without the corresponding platform and content innovations. In short, progress in the information industry now requires close partnerships.

Companies in the computer industry have functioned in this type of partnership model for the last decade. During this time, we have made the transition from an industry that was dominated by vertically integrated players offering solutions that were often proprietary to a horizontally stratified one in which the players specialize in one or a few aspects of the total solution. In today's computer industry, the processor vendors, operating systems vendors, applications developers, and platform vendors all are highly interdependent. This model is being extended rapidly outside the computer industry to include all elements of the information industry. The real winners in this change have been the customers. They now enjoy a multiplicity of services and products, based on open standards, and offered at ever-lower prices.

STAGED TRANSITION

The popular vision of the 500-channel, high-bandwidth highway into the home has received an inordinate amount of attention in the press. I believe this vision is incorrect because it embraces a "couch-potato model" of the consumer and therefore misses the fundamental promise and essential appeal of what is possible.

Recent studies suggest that the cost of installing high-bandwidth service are prohibitive—as much as $2,000 per home. To date, experimental offerings of video-on-demand and home-shopping-type applications show that consumers are unwilling to spend what is needed to justify the investment. The most educated consumers, who can afford to pay, are the least interested in a steady diet of passive movie entertainment.

At the same time, 28% of American households have PCs, people are subscribing to online services and using the Internet at an astonishing pace, and sales of multimedia PCs have exploded. The number of new users of Internet is increasing at the rate of 10 percent per month. Remarkable applications are being developed and utilized in the areas of health care, education, government, and business, all based on today's infrastructure. Customers are using the widely available narrow-band technology and a PC with a modem and CD-ROM drive for communication, information access and dissemination, transaction-oriented tasks, and various "edutainment" activities. The compelling aspect of these applications is their interactivity. This is the element that is grossly underestimated in the couch-potato view, which promotes an array of one-way downloads of linear entertainment and advertisements to a passive consumer whose options are limited to ordering a pizza and a video.

Connectivity will allow users to participate actively in communities of interest. Online services and the Internet provide links for chatting and information sharing that are easily accessed and can be precisely focused to the user's particular interests. Children who have been brought up with interactive games are especially drawn to this type of application. They use the technology to connect to others around the world. Parents report that children will spend hours chatting online, playing interactive games, and accessing various network resources. These same children are bored by passive television. A recent study cited in the *Wall Street Journal* reported that the amount of TV viewing declines in homes that subscribe to an online service such as America Online, CompuServe, or Prodigy. These young customers of tomorrow view the computer as a portal to a connected life in which a computer-chat pal in Japan is as normal as a friend across the street. It appears that many of the adults developing passive systems do not understand the key perceptual and behavioral differences that are now shaping our children.

These factors suggest that the development of the information infrastructure will proceed in measured stages. We will develop and use information technology applications in layers, starting with basic networked services. The evolution will be driven by applications that provide new levels of interactivity and connectivity rather than applications that are simple extrapolations of the passive models of the past. Instead of one or two individual "killer applications" attracting users to the information highway, a large number of diverse applications that touch many different parts of our lives will drive the demand for incrementally higher and higher levels of bandwidth and service from the infrastructure.

THE PC WILL LEAD THE WAY

Many people believe that the TV will be the focus for all services in the home. I doubt that will be the case. Today's TV is an old analog design that receives broadcast signals and displays them using interlace scan. This is hardly a device designed to accommodate the digital world. I believe the PC will play the central role in the NII because it is a multifunctional platform that is well-suited to the mosaic of uses that people are demanding. A PC in the home can be used as a node on the office network, an educational tool for children, a tool for managing personal finances, the place to play entertaining CD-ROMs, as well as a connection to the Internet. The platform is open to all kinds of hardware and software additions and upgrades. These factors make the PC, as it is currently configured, the platform of choice for the near term. One might say the PC is the "ultimate driving machine" on the information highway.

As the infrastructure develops, the PC will evolve with it. It will take new forms that will be adapted for even broader uses. PCs will be made to fit distinct lifestyle needs and to fit more gracefully into specific environments. For example, one could envision PCs for the living room with a large screen and a wood-grained enclosure or a kitchen PC that has integrated telephony, a sophisticated messaging system, a touch sensitive screen, and links for electronic commerce. We might one day see PCs loaded with CD-ROM reference "jukeboxes" and linked to office computers and databases used for home-based study or a playroom PC with multimedia and "edutainment" peripherals such as joy sticks and virtual reality helmets. Or imagine a home mobile PC with embedded wireless communications and voice recognition used in the yard for how-to applications such as planting flowers or building a deck.

These various devices could be linked to each other via a home local area network (LAN) that would allow individual devices to share components such as software, hard drives, and modems. This home LAN would provide access to the information infrastructure with its array of services. Computers would be linked to other smart products in the home such as security and energy-management systems. The sharing of components across all of these elements would make the cost of the total system competitive with what people are spending today on the various separate devices that provide these functions. Increasingly, what we today call a TV and a PC will merge into the same powerful programmable digital device, and at that point, the TV-versus-PC argument will become moot.

APPLICATIONS OF NII TECHNOLOGIES

What are some of the near-term, practical applications of "highway" technology? Each of the following applications of information and communications technologies could have impressive economic and social benefits.

Health Care

We have had a long debate on health care in this country. One point of agreement is the great potential for streamlining the administrative and service aspects of medical care. Information technology holds great promise for this type of cost reduction and has the potential to improve fundamentally the patient-clinician relationship and allow the patient to be a much more informed and active consumer of health services. Systems are being designed that allow patients to access their own medical records, including information on treatment options. Some health care providers are offering online question-response services and publishing online journals that summarize the latest medical research to make it useful for the average patient. These systems supplement and expand patients' knowledge, allowing them to participate more directly in their care.

Telemedicine is another exciting application. This technology is giving rural communities access to specialists in leading medical centers. Using videoconferencing systems with high-speed, high-resolution imaging, the specialists consult with the doctor in remote locations, review X-rays, interview the patient, and offer their expert advice on treatment options. In places where these systems have been tested, users find that the technology not only brings better medicine to the remote areas, but it also enriches rural doctors' lives by giving them access to the knowledge and counsel of world-class specialists.

Business

The continuing importance of information technology to businesses cannot be overstated. The knowledge and expertise of a company's workforce and the ability to access and mobilize this information are two of the basic elements of competitive advantage in today's marketplace and will probably be the most important determinants of success in the future. Realizing the power of the technology lies in shifting our view of information from something that is stored or resides in specific experts to something that has its greatest value when it is fluid and shared for the purposes of problem solving.

Companies are learning how to get the right products to market faster by using information technology. They are using communication technologies to shorten the distance between groups inside the company and to bring the right teams of experts to bear on a given project. Team members are linked for the duration of the project and are easily redeployed upon completion of their work.

These technologies have revolutionary implications for the structure of organizations. They flatten hierarchies, eliminating levels of middle managers whose role was to gather information and move it up or down the organizational pyramid. The new organizational structures use teams of implementers connected via information networks to those who set policy, thus reducing the need for internal intermediaries. The need for external intermediaries is also reduced. Customers and producers and producers and suppliers are linked more directly, significantly reducing cost and greatly increasing the utility and currency of the information passed back and forth.

Information technology also has the potential to allow a better balance between our home and work lives. Telecommuting allows employees to spend more time at home with their families, and it will benefit the environment as auto exhaust emissions fall with reductions in commuting.

As the infrastructure develops, it will spawn a more efficient operating environment that rewards innovation and high-quality, low-cost products. It will also alter fundamentally many of the current business models. For example, as home shopping on a PC supersedes shopping at the mall or through a catalog, this new channel will earn "rent" for its virtual "shelf space." While it is not clear at this point how the conduit and platform vendors will share this income, we can be certain that providing access to the home shopper will earn a return.

Government

We all believe that many aspects of government are unwieldy, uncoordinated, and expensive. We try repeatedly to reorganize government but fail to get the results we want. Information technology, if applied properly, could be an essential part of the solution. It may even help us return to a more democratic society by bringing people together electronically.

The most notable effort in this arena is the Reinventing Government initiative, championed by Vice President Albert Gore. The initiative, which uses information technology to reduce paperwork and streamline administrative processes, already is starting to show results in terms of greater government efficiency, faster processing, increased accuracy, improved service levels, and reduced administration costs.

The new information technologies are also allowing the government to provide new potentially valuable services. For example, the Department of Commerce collects and makes available online reams of market data that companies can use to operate in a more informed manner. Also exciting is the potential for involving more people in the political process. Information technology can closely link the electorate and the elected at the local, state, and national levels.

Education

The decay of the American educational system is a great social tragedy. It may be the single biggest threat to the future social and economic health of the nation. While the information superhighway will be only part of the solution to this problem, it has a major role to play.

Information technology frees us from the traditional but tired model of learning: an "expert" teacher in the front of a classroom intent on dispensing knowledge to a captive group of students. Information technology encourages other modes of classroom teaching— teachers and students do not have to be in the same place at the same time, and learning does not have to stop when the student joins the workforce but can occur throughout one's life.

For example, the National Technological University (NTU), a collaborative effort by a number of leading schools of engineering, is using a satellite TV system to bring the best teachers into corporations around the country. This is extremely affordable for corporations, and it minimizes or eliminates travel time for professors. Equally exciting benefits are becoming available to young learners. In Tennessee, educators are using a network link that allows high school science students to ask questions and get answers from 70 college science professors. This capability complements learning in the classroom.

Teachers themselves are benefiting. Incorporating information technology in the pursuit of learning frees teachers from having to know it all. Instead, they can be facilitators, helping students in their quest for learning. Taking this approach, many teachers find the classroom a less intimidating place.

Technology is helping teachers in other ways as well. In Texas, teachers in remote locations are linked via the Texas Educational Network. They use the network to share lesson plans and ideas on new ways to teach old subjects. In the process, they enrich both their work experience and their students' learning. The same network offers similar advantages in the administrative area.

With increasing cost pressures in academia and the demand for ongoing education in an information-based society, information technology provides an innovative, less-costly way to meet the nation's educational needs.

Entertainment

The implications of new information technologies for entertainment can be profound, but the vision of what might be has been clouded by a focus on a passive rather than interactive model. The interactivity offered by new technologies will allow networked games, full-motion feeds of customized videos, and virtual reality experiences, all available in the home. Either these services will be available using narrow-band technology with processing and compression to allow a near-wideband experience, or they will wait until the investment in higher bandwidth communication is economically justified.

In the near term, communities of interest will meet in cyberspace to interact and enhance each other's knowledge. This new form of entertainment and social activity is the likely forerunner of the entertainment world to come. No couches here.

GUIDING PRINCIPLES FOR GOING FORWARD

Moving forward will require us to overcome various technical challenges. However, the products and services that are on hand today, combined with the technical innovations that will be available shortly, will provide most of the core technology needed to realize the next stage. The more pressing challenges are to identify the embodiments of technology that the consumer will find truly compelling and to ensure the creation and protection of a commercial and academic environment conducive to real innovation.

Meeting these challenges requires the development of responsible public policy. As Vice President Gore stated in a September 1994 speech:

> "Government has an indisputable and appropriate role in developing the GII. By reducing the regulatory barriers and promoting private sector involvement, by identifying the public interests that must be served, and by aggressively using the GII to provide education, health care and other public services, governments can play a key role in developing the GII in cooperation with industry and others in the private sector."

His emphasis on reducing regulatory barriers and on the strong role of the private sector is correct. Untangling the regulatory legacy of the telecommunications and cable industries is critical. These efforts should be directed at opening up access to the networks and to the devices that interface to the networks. We cannot permit telecommunication companies to reassert a de facto monopoly power over access to the home or the equipment used in the home. Nor can we allow the cable companies to act as rigid gatekeepers controlling the content of services they provide. If the conduit providers are allowed to assert monopoly control over access to the home, or if they are directed to do so in the name of universal service, this will seriously stifle progress in the development of the infrastructure.

The government will also need to work to assure interoperability. Here we should encourage straightforward, open standards whose effect is to encourage competition among compatible solutions. The opportunity for missteps is significant. For example, the idea of requiring interoperability not only with new technologies but also with all antecedent systems is potentially paralyzing. There are already many industry, national, and international organizations that have a long history of debating, creating, and promulgating standards for information technology. We do not need to impose another or higher-level standards-setting process. Finally, forcing standards that are too rigid or pervasive risks locking in inferior, unworkable, and uneconomical approaches.

We must also avoid pressures to turn this into a government entitlement program. Because the Clinton administration has shown such a strong interest in this issue, some parties are recommending poorly conceived technical visions in hopes of winning government funding for ill-considered research activities that tend to complicate fairly simple facts and practices. They suggest problems that exist only in the minds of over-reaching central planners and over-zealous academics. Let's not overstudy this, particularly in an academic vacuum.

Many individuals advocate universal service to ensure that we do not stratify our society into "information haves and have nots." They promote special support for needy individuals to allow them access to the information infrastructure. Careful thought should be applied to the priority we place on information access relative to other needs in our society. In our zeal to provide access to advanced information services for individuals, we must be careful not to place higher value on the highway than we place on food, shelter, and basic medical care.

Adherents of universal access look to the health care, education, and government sectors to support widespread involvement in the information infrastructure. This is a worthy objective, but I recommend we examine closely the rationale and methods for such funding. John Browning, in a superb article in the September 1994 *Wired* magazine, writes:

> "Universal service cross-subsidies are a tax—albeit a tax buried in the price of services and beneath layers of obscure allocation and pricing regulation. They are a particularly inefficient and wasteful tax. And worst of all, they are a deceptive and distorting tax, a tax that makes it hard to see the real costs of the building blocks of tomorrow's networks and thus the real opportunities in building the networks that will change the world."

Since health, education, and government represent a sizable proportion of our economy, this tax would be substantial, could obscure the true costs of providing a specific service, and as a result could hinder and distort the development of this enterprise. In general, the less subsidy, the better. We should subsidize the consumer, not the provider.

CONCLUSION

A free-market approach to the development of the infrastructure is critical to the appropriate development of products and services. This point of view was strongly supported in a 1994 report issued by European Union Commissioner Martin Bangemann that led to the Commission's recent "action plan." Allowing market forces to guide the computer industry, and more recently the telephone industry, has worked well for industry, government, and the consumer. The Internet is an excellent demonstration of what can be achieved through unconstrained, unregulated innovation. With a minimum of government funding and a lot of collaboration between government and academia—and most of all by letting a balance develop between what people want and what they are free to supply—the Internet has grown and will continue to develop at an astonishing pace. The Internet points to a future in which the information infrastructure is not a highway but a web of interrelated public and private networks, platforms, and services. A market approach will allow the infrastructure to continue to grow while addressing real needs today, will create an atmosphere that encourages experimentation and rapid learning, and will permit good ideas to flourish and bad ideas to die.

A word of caution: we must not underestimate the population of future users. By this I mean we should not develop the NII and all the related products with an inactive user in mind. What is exciting is not the ability to deliver more passive entertainment products. Instead, the focus should be on new forms of entertainment, new connections, and new ways of learning.

The NII is based on technologies in which American industry leads the world. If we creatively pursue this opportunity with the right goals in mind, there will be significant benefits to both the public and private sectors. Moreover, we will lead the world into a new and truly exciting era.

Satellite Communications in the Global Information Infrastructure

STEVEN D. DORFMAN

This paper presents my views on satellite communications and the global information infrastructure (GII). I believe the GII is more important to the future of this country in terms of world leadership, job creation, and export revenues than the national information infrastructure (NII), which is often called the information superhighway. The GII is also of paramount importance to the world's newly emerging global economy. Today's global marketplace requires a reliable, timely, and unrestricted flow of people, information, capital, and products. By creating a seamless, ubiquitous, and cost-efficient global information infrastructure, we provide the communications architecture for the global marketplace. Satellites, in particular, will play a critical role in executing this mission.

THE NATIONAL INFORMATION INFRASTRUCTURE

Ever since Vice President Albert Gore first lit the fuse with his focus on the NII, the media have responded with a barrage of stories. Media megamergers, alliances, and acquisitions are frequent news. Stock prices soar at the mention of the magic phrase "interactive multimedia." Conferences are being held, and committees are being formed. Hundreds of billions of dollars have been pledged to build the NII.

Much of this interest is justified, because we are indeed on the brink of turning some fascinating concepts into reality. These include viewing whatever we want, whenever we want—video on demand; strolling through video shopping malls from our living room and ordering with a push of a button on the remote control; having two-way fiber optic video transmission into and out of the home; playing video games with someone in another state; telemedicine; and telecommuting.

But so far, most of what we hear and read about the NII suggests that fiber will be the delivery system. Satellites are seldom mentioned. Even the term "information superhighway" connotes something that is land-based, which is why I believe this term is a misnomer. It is true we already have 15 million miles of fiber optic cable crisscrossing the country. This is more than 300 times the mileage of our federal interstate highway system. However, I believe that satellites will play a major role in the NII, because they fulfill both of Vice President Gore's clearly stated NII policy objectives of competition and universal access.

COMPETITION AND UNIVERSAL ACCESS IN THE NII

The real story behind the hype about the NII is competition—how we are breaking away from the monopoly concept of telephone and cable service. The original thought that government would invest huge sums to help create the information superhighway is gone. Instead, telecommunication bills are being promoted to encourage competition for local phone, cable, and long-distance service. Now, the cable company will be able to compete with the local phone company and vice versa, while long-distance and local phone companies will also be able to compete with one another. In this competitive environment, prices will drop, services will improve, and new applications will flourish.

Regarding universal access, the second NII policy goal, the real issue here is the last-mile link to the home or office. This final mile, bridged either by wire or by satellite dish, is where the majority of costs are.

THE ECONOMICS OF SATELLITE TRANSMISSION

Satellite communications will flourish in this new competitive environment and will help make universal access a reality. Hughes' newly launched DIRECTV service is a good example. We offer 150 channels of TV service to homes that have no cable. That is universal access. We also provide a competitive alternative to consumers who do have access to cable. While bridging the last mile to the home by cable costs $2000, providing this link by satellite costs $700. The economics favor satellites, if the playing field is kept level by preventing cross subsidies.

Similarly, satellite communication will provide two-way, high data-rate services using very small aperture terminals (VSATs) where Integrated Services Digital Network (ISDN) is not readily available, and it will be a competitive alternative where ISDN is available. Moreover, satellites can provide mobile communication when terrestrial cellular communication is unavailable.

Thus, with 20 gigahertz (GHz) of satellite transmission capacity available from geostationary orbit, a new realism is now replacing the hype. Many are now questioning whether the cost of a fiber to each home is justified if phone users or taxpayers do not pay for it. After all, how much are people willing to pay to save a trip to the local video store, especially when a service like DIRECTV can provide video on near demand?

As a result, alliances and mergers, such as the one between Bell Atlantic and TCI, are being reconsidered. Pilot interactive multimedia systems are being carefully reviewed, and investments are being rethought. One Bell Atlantic executive recently described the firm's planned advanced video networks as "a little more difficult to develop than people thought." The company intends to invest $11 billion to develop these networks.

Like other companies, Hughes is working vigorously to inject the already sophisticated NII with new capabilities and services that focus on satellite communications. I am particularly proud of our Galaxy Classroom project, where we have demonstrated the power of satellite-based distance learning by accelerating the learning rate of K–4 students by one grade in 40 schools around the country. We will expand this program to 20,000 schools. We support the efforts of Congress, the Justice Department, and the Federal Communications

Commission (FCC) as they strive to implement the architecture that will serve this country best in the 21st century.

Increasingly, however, Hughes is also focusing its attention outside the United States. As both industrialized and developing nations increase their demand for access to information, entertainment, and mobile communications, the GII is where the action will be. In a March 21, 1994 speech in Buenos Aires, Vice President Gore talked about the importance of the GII and did an excellent job of positioning America for a leadership role. The ubiquitous reach of satellites—their ability to provide that crucial last-mile link—means that satellite technology will play a major role in the GII.

THE GII: MEETING THE WORLD'S NEED FOR TELECOMMUNICATIONS

In recent years, the world has exchanged a bipolar, Cold War mentality for an environment that recognizes the benefits of multilateral trade and cultural exchange. A global economy has emerged. But developing nations are finding that in order to participate in this global economy, they must build significant infrastructure—everything from modern roads and air transportation systems to reliable electronic banking and telecommunications networks.

A global information infrastructure will require massive development around the world. Many countries have only minimal access to communications technologies and very primitive or poorly developed internal and external connectivity. China, for example, will spend $600 billion on infrastructure in the next 6 years. Without huge spending on such infrastructure, developing nations will experience bottlenecks that will impede their economic growth and social progress. Ironically, because they have made limited investments in communications infrastructure in the past, developing countries will be heavy users of wireless, digital, and satellite technologies.

PRIVATIZATION, COMPETITION, AND ADVANCES IN SATELLITE TECHNOLOGY

As we move toward a seamless, ubiquitous, and cost-efficient global information network, three significant trends are shaping the future of satellite communications.

The first is privatization. Many governments cannot readily afford the major investments required to develop communications infrastructure and so are increasingly turning to sources of private capital. In Latin America, privatization is revolutionizing telecommunications in places like Mexico, Argentina, Chile, Colombia, and Venezuela. In 1994, India ended its state monopoly on telecommunications after determining it would have had to spend over $7 billion to modernize its phone system.

As privatization takes hold, Hughes' international satellite construction business is becoming increasingly commercial. For instance, most of the satellites we now build for other countries are contracted by private firms. Hughes-built satellites serving Japan, Malaysia, China, Indonesia, Luxembourg, and Thailand were all contracted by private, nongovernment entities.

Competition is the second key trend shaping the future of satellite communications. Competition from both domestic and foreign satellite service providers is driving down costs, spurring technological innovation, improving service, and expanding offerings to users.

In August 1994, for example, Singapore announced it would let privately owned companies compete to provide satellite communications links that previously could be supplied only by two government-controlled enterprises. By 1998, the European Union will deregulate all basic telecommunication services, opening a $100 billion-a-year market to competition.

Privatization and competition are also creating new regional satellite operators, like Panamsat and SES. With the launch of PAS-3 in December 1994 and PAS-4 in 1995—both high-power Hughes 601 satellites—Panamsat will operate the world's first privately owned global satellite system. SES, based in Luxembourg, covers Europe with high-power TV signals using HS601 satellites. Private companies like SES and Panamsat are building and expanding their systems to compete against the old-line public satellite consortia. Along with added capacity, these new operators are infusing the international satellite transmission market with greater flexibility, improved performance, and competitive pricing.

The third factor shaping the future of satellite communication and, along the way, helping to create a more universal and lower-cost global information infrastructure, is the quantum leap that has been achieved in satellite technology. Improvements in efficiency in space, on the ground, and within the radio spectrum are lowering the cost of satellites and satellite services for everyone. For example, 30 years ago one needed a 100-foot antenna to receive one TV channel from a satellite, but today's DIRECTV can transmit 150 TV channels into an 18-inch dish.

ADVANCES IN SATELLITES, EARTH TERMINALS, AND DIGITAL TECHNOLOGY

Let us take a closer look at some of these technological advances. Today's satellites are more powerful and efficient. Reconfigurable spot-beam antennas shape the beams more accurately and weigh less. Miniaturization and component improvements have made receivers more sensitive and lighter. Traveling-wave tubes and solid-state power amplifiers have increased efficiency and, hence, require less prime power. Batteries and solar panels are more efficient and lighter. Microprocessors simplify tracking, telemetry, and control of the satellite. Modern composite techniques contribute to lighter-weight satellite structures, and on-board propulsion has become more cost-effective. In 1995, Hughes will launch the first commercial ion-propulsion system, for the Galaxy III-R spacecraft. This will save 800 pounds of satellite mass and more than $10 million per launch. As a result of these technological improvements and improved production efficiency, the Hughes 601 satellite is up to five times more cost-effective than its predecessor of the 1980s.

Advances in technology are also yielding more efficient, lower-cost ground-based satellite terminals. At the 1977 World Administrative Radio Conference, scientists predicted that 60 decibel watts (dBW) of power would be required to transmit TV signals to a one-meter dish. Since then, there has been great improvement in receiver sensitivity, antenna efficiency, and signal processing. Today, only 50 dBW are required to transmit TV to a half-meter dish, and receivers can be purchased for less than $700.

Finally, digital communication combined with digital data compression is enabling new satellite applications. For example, compression of digital audio signals has made satellite mobile communications economically feasible by increasing the capacity of satellites tenfold. Compression of digital video signals will result in at least a fivefold increase in the capacity of a transponder to transmit television channels. This, combined with the decreased cost of decompression chip sets in ground receivers, permits new applications of satellite digital TV, such as Hughes' DIRECTV. In general, compression of digital signals will significantly reduce the cost of transmitting through satellites. I believe that the satellite communication market is elastic and that the reduced cost will increase demand.

AN EXPLOSION OF SATELLITE COMMUNICATIONS

We already see evidence that the increased cost-efficiency of satellite communications is stimulating demand. There is an abundance of new satellite capacity. Already, 145 commercial communications satellites orbit the globe. Another two dozen were scheduled for launch during the last three months of 1994, and more than 100 new commercial communications satellites are on order. Nine hundred filings have been submitted to the International Telecommunication Union (ITU) for future satellite systems, and that number excludes hundreds more low Earth-orbiting (LEO) satellites that companies such as Iridium and Teledesic plan to launch. At Hughes, we have our largest-ever backlog; in 1994 and 1995, we will be launching an average of one satellite per month for customers in Thailand, Mexico, Brazil, and other countries.

The technological advances I described—more powerful satellites, more sensitive lower-cost receivers, and digital communications—are bringing more than just cost efficiencies. They are also stimulating new satellite applications. I would like to discuss three of these: high-speed interactive voice, data, and video transmission; satellite mobile services, which will eventually evolve into hand-held terminals; and direct-to-home television broadcasting through satellites.

Before discussing high-speed interactive communications, however, we must consider that much of the world is still in need of basic telephony. In China, which has fewer than two phone lines for every 100 citizens, a private residential phone line from the Beijing Telephone Company requires a 6 month wait and costs $575, the average government worker's salary for an entire year. In Mexico, the phone system is so unreliable that when a call finally does go through, the common greeting is not "Hello" but "Who have I reached?"

Satellites, in the form of VSAT networks, already play a tremendous role in providing basic telephony in such areas. While voice is not a common VSAT application in the developed world, it is perhaps the most critical application in both public and private networks in places such as China, India, southern Asia, and Eastern Europe. VSATs also transmit two-way data and video for business applications and offer the unique ability to overcome the challenges posed by distance and terrain.

In Africa, for example, 70 percent of the people live in rural areas, and major business centers, like Cairo and Nairobi, are thousands of miles apart. The continent's vast mountain and desert areas would make it prohibitively expensive to provide telephony via fixed terrestrial links. VSATs offer an immediate, low-cost solution and the only real opportunity to rapidly advance the continent's economic development. It will be a very long time before the developing countries of the world have fiber optic networks approaching the sophisticated networks that exist in the United States.

VSAT networks are providing far more than basic public telephone and government communications services. They're also being used for more sophisticated applications in banking, retail merchandising, oil exploration, and newspaper production and distribution. In Europe, VSATs handle Holiday Inn's international reservations system and Visa's global transaction network. The *China People's Daily* is published via a VSAT network.

SPACEWAY: HIGH DATA RATES AND BANDWIDTH ON DEMAND

With these VSAT applications as a starting point, we now find ourselves on the threshold of a new era of interactive high data-rate transmission. Microsoft's Bill Gates and cellular phone pioneer Craig McCaw made headlines when they announced an ambitious plan to launch a high data-rate global satellite business, Teledesic. The project would rely on a global network of 840 low Earth-orbiting satellites.

Alternatively, Hughes has announced its intention to establish a global network of geostationary (GEO) satellites, called Spaceway, that will provide an interactive bandwidth-on-demand service for telephony, high-speed data exchange, and high-resolution interactive video. Spaceway will consist of four interconnected regional satellite systems operating in the Ka band and providing worldwide coverage. By transmitting in this high frequency band and by using tightly focused spot beams, we can transmit to or from ultra-small antennas measuring 26 inches in diameter. The price of these dishes will be less than $1,000.

The Spaceway system will play two key roles. First, it will provide basic telephony to underserved areas of the world and offer these regions access to global telecommunication. Second, Spaceway will provide critical advanced communications support to the global marketplace, where huge quantities of information must be accessed and shared electronically.

Spaceway will offer business users a wide variety of applications, including desktop video telephony and conferencing, computer networking, technical tele-imaging, CAD/CAM transmission, and high-speed, low-cost access to the next generation of online multimedia databases, at rates from 16 kilobits per second to 1.5 megabits per second, and higher if necessary.

Spaceway will enable the entire world to have access to the kind of souped-up capacity that we are planning for the United States. And, it will deliver capacity on demand using asynchronous transfer mode (ATM) technology at a relatively low cost. Spaceway will offer two-way video for less than the current price of an international phone call and international phone calls for less than the current price of a local phone call.

THE NEXT GENERATION:
MOBILE SATELLITE SERVICES

Meanwhile, our second new application—satellite mobile communications—is about to take off. The pioneering work has been done by Inmarsat, which provides service to tens of thousands of maritime and aeronautical customers. The first land mobile services will be available soon via piggybacked payloads on the already-launched Optus and Solidaridad satellites of Australia and Mexico, respectively.

In spring 1995, the first high-power land mobile satellite, AMSC-1, will be launched, followed shortly by its twin, TMI-1. These satellites, which Hughes is building for the U.S. American Mobile Satellite Corporation and the Canadian Telesat Mobile Incorporated, will for the first time give cellular car phone users ubiquitous roaming service across North America. Dual-mode handsets will route calls over cellular networks when they are available and by satellite when they are not.

AMSC-1 and TMI-1 will interconnect with all existing cellular systems and with the entire public switched telephone network, creating the first seamless network for nationwide mobile voice, data, and fax communications in the United States and Canada. The satellites will be capable of serving hundreds of thousands of customers.

A follow-on AMSC-2 satellite with eight times the capacity of AMSC-1 will lower costs; more important, its tightly focused spot beams and on-board digital processing will reduce the needed uplink power to less than one-half watt. This will permit hand-held service, using lightweight pocket phones, for the first time.

Hughes is one of several companies examining hand-held mobile telephone service in other regions of the world—Pacific Asia, for example, where demand is great. While Hughes and others are currently working on geostationary systems, several different entities have proposed projects that would provide worldwide hand-held service via a constellation of either low or medium Earth-orbiting (MEO) satellites.

Two LEO systems are being built: Motorola's 66-satellite Iridium project and the 48-satellite Globalstar system from Loral/Qualcomm. A MEO system based on 12 satellites is planned by Inmarsat. Construction of this system is scheduled to start in 1995.

Each type of system proposed—GEO, LEO, and MEO—has certain advantages. A GEO system is most suitable as a regional system and has the lowest cost. Ultimately, a series of regional GEO systems could form a global system. A LEO system will be the most expensive service because of the large number of satellites required, but it will not have the transmission-time delay of GEO satellites. A MEO system will be more expensive than a GEO but less than a LEO and will have minimal time delay.

I believe worldwide demand will be such that all three types of systems could coexist. Ubiquitous hand-held telephony, using a combination of satellite and terrestrial communications infrastructure, is a virtual certainty for the 21st century.

DIRECT-TO-HOME DIGITAL TV

High-power direct-to-home TV is already a reality. With the launch of Hughes' DBS-1 and DBS-2 satellites, every U.S. household with a TV can now access a cornucopia of digitally pure video programming, accompanied by CD-quality audio, via an 18-inch dish. Using digital compression, Hughes' DIRECTV company and Hubbard's USSB are able to beam more than 150 channels of premium programming directly into every American home. Competitors such as Echostar and Primestar have announced similar services.

Demand for TV entertainment and information is also exploding internationally. Currently, more than 25 million privately owned satellite dishes in backyards and on rooftops across the world are delivering vast menus of programming directly into the home. SES, for example, is broadcasting programs in five languages to over 17 million privately owned receivers. After Germany and the United Kingdom, Poland is the European country that has the largest number of privately owned dishes, even though no Polish language channels are broadcasting and satellite dishes were banned there until 1990. Satellites with names like AsiaSat, APStar, Palapa, JCSat, Superbird, and Astra are sources of such familiar channels as CNN, HBO, ESPN, and MTV.

Because most of the world has access to only a handful of local channels, there is enormous pent-up demand for more variety and for foreign programs. This demand can be filled most cost-effectively by satellite TV, especially when there is little or no cable. As already indicated, it costs less to provide access by satellite than to build a new cable or fiber link to the home.

Because of these fundamental economics and built-in demand, Hughes is exporting its high-power direct broadcast satellite (DBS) technology to the rest of the world. We are building high-power satellites capable of direct-to-home broadcasts for China, Malaysia, Mexico, Australia, and Japan, among others. Australia, which has no cable and only a handful of broadcast stations in the major cities, got its first direct-to-home TV service in 1992 via an Optus satellite. A second Optus satellite went into service in 1994.

Also, Hughes recently teamed up with three of Latin America's leading media companies in a joint venture called Galaxy Latin America (GLA). Beginning in early 1996, GLA will bring multichannel satellite-to-home digital TV to millions of households in Central and South America and the Caribbean. Panamsat has announced a similar system.

The spectacular success of Star-TV in the Asian-Pacific region is a good window into the future of satellite-to-home TV worldwide. Star-TV uses 10 channels on AsiaSat, which Hughes built in 1990, to beam entertainment programming to 60 million homes in 53 countries. Apparently, *The Bold and the Beautiful* and *Santa Barbara* are especially popular in India.

Because of all these satellites, global viewership is rising exponentially. CNN International currently has 80 million subscribers, up from just 11.6 million in October, 1991. Soon, satellites will serve the entire world with direct-to-home digital TV, providing multiple programming choices from every corner of the globe.

A VISION FOR THE FUTURE

In 1962, President John F. Kennedy envisioned the United States using its technology to connect the world through satellite communications. From this vision came the Communications Satellite Act and two of the most successful international organizations in history, Intelsat and Inmarsat.

Now, more than 30 years later, we have the opportunity to transport President Kennedy's vision into the next millennium. By expanding on that vision, we can create a global telecommunications infrastructure that will make this a better world. This satellite-based network will allow schoolchildren in a remote African village to receive a superior academic or technical education from instructors in Nairobi, Cairo, or virtually anywhere in the world. It will enable a doctor in Afghanistan to transmit a patient's X-rays and medical records instantly to a consulting specialist in the United States. Local contractors in Sarajevo or Beirut will be able to rebuild their cities with the benefit of online engineering and architectural expertise from other countries. And, using workgroup computing, employees in the budding economic zones of Eastern Europe can contribute their talents to leading multinational corporations.

An integral part of this global telecommunications infrastructure will be the satellite global phone, which we will automatically slip into our purse or pocket each morning. It will be a smart phone, always in communication with our personal computer, even as we travel to the most remote corners of the world. It will know where we are through a global positioning system (GPS) chip set, automatically switching to satellite mode when we move out of range of terrestrial cells.

Satellite-to-home television will keep us well informed and entertained and will help us learn and understand the values and cultures of other societies. Hundreds of millions of us will own personal satellite dishes, and we will be able to receive programs from every continent. Everybody will be watching news events as they happen, wherever they happen. There will no longer be any remote corners of the world.

There will be challenges. We must modify the Comsat, Intelsat, and Inmarsat organizations so they can keep pace with today's technology and the worldwide drive toward competition and privatization. We must formulate an international approach to the orderly allocation of frequency spectrum for geostationary and low Earth-orbiting satellites in a highly competitive marketplace. Sufficient spectrum exists for all of the satellite applications discussed here, but it must be allocated efficiently. Another challenge we face is to create a global environment that permits the free flow of information across borders and, at the same time, protects copyrights.

As in 1962, we have an enormous opportunity to shape the future of satellite communications around the world. By exporting our nation's rich store of satellite technology and know-how, we not only create new jobs in the United States and boost our own economy, we also further the economic and social progress of developing nations through improved access to education and health care. By exporting America's defining values of democracy and human rights, we will make this a better world.

Current Trends and Likely Futures in Wireless Systems

JOHN E. MAJOR

No matter how you look at it, the 1990s has been an incredible period for communications in general and wireless communications in particular. For example, the paging industry, once predicted to be eclipsed by the cellular industry, is now growing faster than ever. By the end of 1993, there were some 50 million pagers in use worldwide; 150 million units may be in service by the turn of the century. That is 150 million units for a service that was expected just several years ago to pass out of use. Meanwhile, cellular communication and now Personal Communications Services (PCS) have exploded onto the world scene. Although there were just 600,000 units in service at the end of 1985, some 33 million units were in service worldwide at the end of 1993, and the prediction is for well over 100 million cellular and PCS units by the year 2000.

Moving beyond sales figures, governments worldwide have embraced the issue of communications, and wireless communications in particular, as a national priority. The U.S. government stimulated this trend when it began using two new acronyms, NII (National Information Infrastructure) and GII (Global Information Infrastructure). Neither the NII nor the GII is fully developed yet, but open debate about them at the national and international level has focused attention on important issues and helped accelerate the process of change.

Although this is a global story, one can gain an understanding of it by focusing on events in the United States. In 1994, the Federal Communications Commission (FCC) allocated 3 megahertz (MHz) of spectrum for a new class of service called narrow-band PCS—paging, if you will. That move doubled the available spectrum and opened up the potential for whole new classes of services. For example, one will be able to know that a page was received, and because the network will be able to locate the cell the pager is in, it will be economical to send much longer pages, such as the day's agenda. Finally, the person being paged will be able to respond with short messages such as, "I'll reach you this evening."

Following narrow-band PCS is PCS itself, which is essentially upbanded cellular communication.[1] For this service, 120 MHz of spectrum has been set aside, which is more than twice what was previously available. This not only makes possible truly competitive cellular service, with the attendant benefits of decreasing costs and increasing features, but it also offers the prospect of enhanced voice quality for a wireless last-mile alternative that would provide competition in the local loop. The FCC has allocated another 20 MHz of spectrum for unlicensed PCS to be used for building networks and wireless local area networks (LANs). Finally, some 33 MHz has been designated for use by big LEOs, or low Earth-orbiting satellite networks, to provide global wireless service.

All of this—the 3-, 120-, 20-, and 33-MHz allocations—has occurred in just 2 years' time. Similar activities are under way around the world. The pace is startling, and if we proceed with courage, energy, and vision, we can expect much more to happen as the decade proceeds.

The outcome of these trends depends greatly on what we choose to do, for there are still many unresolved issues in the NII/GII debate. These include concerns about security and privacy, interoperability, information access, ease of use, portability, ubiquity, network availability and manageability, applications development, and network components. This paper will focus on just two of these: portability and ubiquity. Unless the NII/GII initiative satisfies these two re-

---

[1] Upbanded cellular communication is cellular service at the 1.8-gigahertz (GHz) band. Today's service is at the 800-MHz band.

quirements, it cannot deliver the promised convenience, services, and applications.

INDIVIDUAL VOICE AND PUBLIC IMAGES

After some 100 years of technological progress in telecommunications, we live in a world that can be characterized as having "individual voice" and "public images." Individual voice means that almost anyone can have a voice conversation with almost anyone else, anywhere, at any time. With cellular and cordless technologies, the phones are locally or regionally wireless, and the wireless network that supports them is implemented by a highly complementary parallel wired network. There are some limitations in terms of access, costs, and competition, but recent PCS decisions will greatly improve these areas.

Ours is a world of public images because those broadband, or video-based, services are still comparatively expensive or controlled tightly. Whereas anyone can make a phone call, only those with specialized equipment and an FCC license can broadcast a television show or movie. Further, in this world of individual voice and public images, information and computing have largely been left out of the technological picture. Newspapers, books, and learning services are obtained pretty much as they were at the turn of the century—in newsstands, libraries, and schools.

The NII/GII initiative holds the potential to change dramatically all of this and in so doing to empower all citizens through the opportunities that result from making communication services personally accessible. In the NII/GII vision, the separate worlds of individual voice and public images will be unified. That is, individuals will have full access not to just voice services, as they do today, but also to image-based and information services that can now only be imagined. This is telecommunications with full mobility and connectivity, and it will be made possible by completing the second- and third-generation systems that must be part of the global telecommunications agenda.

A VISION AT RISK

The promise of NII/GII lies in three synergistic forces: the availability of bandwidth resulting from developments in fiber optics and signaling; the availability of computing brought on by the development of the microprocessor and advances in semiconductor technology; and the emergence of competition and choice spawned by new telecommunications policies worldwide.

What is missing from this picture is wireless communications, the next generation of telecommunication technology represented by paging, cellular, and PCS services. Until recently, everything you could receive on a wall-attached television in your home, you could receive on a portable television, whether you chose to use it in another room, on a campout, or at a sporting event. That started to change with cable, when the delivered wired bandwidth for television services was effectively increased by two orders of magnitude. Today, one buys a portable TV but ends up tying it permanently to the wall with a coaxial line. That has got to change.

A similar shift has occurred in computing. Early on, what could be done with a portable computer, or what we then called a portable computer, was pretty much what could be done with an office or home computer. That changed when LANs and computer networks came into being. With that transition, the unnetworked portable computer became less useful than its LAN-based equivalent. These changes initially went unnoticed; after all, at least the new portable computer was portable when you carried it home. This too will change. In the near future, for a portable computer to be truly portable, the network will need to be portable as well.

Let us keep this perspective and move forward to the time when the NII/GII begins to deliver on its promises. People far from one another will be able to talk face to face, so groups can interact and decisions made more quickly; families will be united although they live miles apart; and high-speed computing and information access will be available in the home and office. Because of these developments, people will be more productive and better informed. Today, the communications services that are available to a worker in his or her office are available when that person is on the move. In the future, that will no longer be true unless broadband wireless services are brought in line with broadband wired services.

Some people say this cannot be done. Can you imagine what would have happened to television if, when it was first conceptualized, people had said that it would not work because it could not be made to fit into the bandwidth of the existing AM and FM radio channels? It took great courage and vision to make the changes necessary to support television. Similar vision and courage are necessary to develop broadband wireless networks.

This picture of broadband wireless communication of the future prompts two questions: Does having wireless matter? If it does, can this future be realized with the technology now available and despite other likely constraints? The answer to both questions is "yes." Already, we have seen the high value people put on mobility. That demand for mobility is generating vast new high-growth industries that produce products to make our citizens more accessible and our companies more efficient. Substantial new export markets are opening up for these products.

APPLICATIONS OF MOBILE COMMUNICATIONS

What I have just outlined is the broad picture, but what happens in specific circumstances and industries is perhaps more important. The availability and dependability of private land-mobile communications is one of the primary factors that has allowed the United States to establish and maintain its position as the world's leading producer of goods and services. Private land-mobile radio is used by all segments of the industrial, business, public-safety, public-service, and land-transportation workforces. The continued growth of this nation's commercial and public-service activities demands additional communication capabilities. It is imperative that the industrial and public-safety sectors have access to new imaging and decision-processing/remote-file access technologies. Even though personal communications services will be available to the general public through common and private carriers, public-safety, public-service, and industrial users will continue to satisfy their specialized communications requirements through private systems.

A community of private land-mobile radio users is necessary to maintain global competitiveness. Motivated by the constant need to improve productivity and service, private users will invariably migrate to the specific communications solutions that provide the greatest advantage to their operations. An additional allocation of radio spectrum is essential if these users and their industries are to continue to flourish in increasingly competitive global markets.

Wireless systems will serve the critical day-to-day operational needs of a variety of industrial, public-safety, and public-service sectors. These include:

Law Enforcement

- Mobile transmission of fingerprints, mug shots, warrants, and other images to and from law enforcement field personnel
- Mobile transmission of maps, floor layouts, and architectural drawings for crime-in-progress operations
- Tactical use of live mobile video for hostage, arrest, and surveillance operations
- High-resolution graphics and electronic transfer of maps and other graphic information to police vehicles
- Vehicle- and personnel-tracking systems
- Wireless "dog tag" locator services to help assure personnel security
- On-board information and security systems for mass transit vehicles

Energy Conservation and Management

- Advanced distribution automation, such as remote monitoring, coordination, and operation of distribution and transmission components from centralized locations, for load management, advanced metering, and system-control functions
- Demand-side management (DSM) systems; for example, managing the consumption of electric power and natural gas
- Transmissions to monitor and record pipeline flow and pipeline pressure indicators
- Real-time monitoring, alerting, and control in situations involving handling of hazardous materials

Health Care and Fire/Emergency Medical Systems

- Remote monitoring of patients' vital signs in health-care facilities to allow immediate response in the event of a patient medical crisis
- Mobile transmission of maps, floor layouts, and architectural drawings to assist fire fighters and other response personnel in the rescue of individuals in emergencies

- Transmission of visual signals and physician instructions in support of rescue operations
- High-speed transmission of high-resolution medical imagery and data from paramedics to hospitals
- Automated inventory control

Pollution Control

- High-resolution graphics and electronic transfer of maps and other graphics information to mobile users
- Management and remediation operations following spills or other crises
- Real-time monitoring, alerting, and control in situations involving handling of hazardous materials
- Visual inspection of pipes and cables exposed during excavation projects

Industrial Productivity

- Automatic transmission of messages advising of impending shortages of parts in a manufacturing environment
- Vehicle and personnel tracking systems
- Locator service based on wireless transmitters to address personnel security
- Remote safety and security inspection of inaccessible locations
- Automation of process- and quality-control functions
- Transmission of scheduling and cost updates, job site inspection results, and performance assessments relating to construction projects
- Wireless "face-to-face" conferences between in-house production and sales personnel

Intelligent Vehicle Highway Systems (IVHS)

- Traffic management systems that adjust to actual traffic conditions rather than rely on historical patterns
- Systems that can electronically weigh and inspect commercial vehicles in motion, issue and monitor permits, or track a container throughout a multimodal shipment

- Systems that permit electronic collection of tolls and transit fares
- Devices that alert authorities to the need for emergency vehicles at the site of a collision or other roadside situation

The recent spectrum allocation for PCS will not satisfy the personal-use needs for emerging wireless technologies. The regulatory scheme adopted for PCS makes it impractical, if not impossible, for private users to obtain and use their own PCS licenses for the new telecommunications technologies they need. Private users, including those in public-safety fields, need to use continuously the spectrum allocated to them so that they can design systems to meet specific needs. Consider two examples. First, for the typical PCS user, radio coverage while in a building or even in a basement might be desirable, but it is not critical. If a portable phone does not work in these locations, it is an inconvenience but no more. However, for a fire fighter trapped in the basement of a burning building, that same lack of coverage could be a life and death matter. Systems only deliver this type of coverage throughout a service area if they are specifically designed to do so. Second, if a system does not work during very adverse conditions—a flood, an ice storm, or a power blackout—it is again just an inconvenience for the typical PCS user. This is not true for the radio systems used by certain crucial components of our infrastructure. Phone and utility companies, for instance, design such systems to work regardless of emergency conditions. In fact, the functioning of these systems is critical during such emergencies.

PHASED APPROACH

One aspect of the NII/GII vision calls for fully mobile communications. Implementation of this goal should take place in two phases; the first requires immediate attention, and the second requires specific actions toward deployment by the turn of the century.

Phase I

Spectrum allocations for second-generation LEO satellite systems for hand-held, two-way subscriber units and pagers. Although the first generation of LEO technology is only now being brought to market, it is not too early to plan additional spectrum allocations in anticipation of LEO's success. An additional 60 MHz will be required to allow for the expansion of existing systems and the emergence of anticipated competitive systems.

Spectrum allocations for industrial and public-safety digital systems with broadband capability. It has always been a priority of the FCC to ensure that all necessary spectra critical to public safety and industry support are made available. As such, the long tradition of support and forward-looking solutions for public safety and private industry has been marked by the continued leadership of the United States. To prepare for the next series of changes, it is estimated that 75 MHz of spectrum will be needed to deliver digital systems with broadband capability. These systems will not support continuous full-motion video, but they will allow selected slow-scan video, image transmissions, file searches, and the transmission of building layouts, maps identifying the locations of hazardous chemicals, and fingerprints.

IVHS. One function of the information highway is to support and make more efficient existing physical roadways through IVHS programs. These programs need additional spectra to support the transfer of information between vehicles and IVHS infrastructure. Twenty MHz is needed to meet this requirement.

Phase II

Analog cellular, paging, and private systems provided the first generation of wireless communications. The second generation consists of digital systems, such as U.S. Digital Cellular (USDC), that remined existing systems, PCS, and the first phase of the NII mobility initiatives. Third-generation systems for private or public use allow paging, or image data, or voice transmission with similar functionality but with flexible broadband capability, increased capacity, satellite system interconnectivity, and global roaming. These systems not only support data, but they support it at LAN rates. They deliver the full capacity of the NII/GII vision to the mobile person. Clearly, a substantial amount of spectrum will need to be set aside to support competing public systems, wireless cable access, and private systems with this capacity. Efforts are just beginning to assess spectrum use and availability around the world.

THE ROLE FOR THE GOVERNMENT

How can government help? First and foremost, the government needs to accept what history has shown—that mobility is essential. Wireless solutions need to be an explicit part of the NII/GII agenda. The initial 155 MHz should be for industrial and public-safety services, IVHS, and satellite services. Substantial additional spectrum will be required to support third-generation systems. Government assistance needs to be focused on making spectrum available. Remining of portions of the spectrum used by broadcast television should be considered in light of the capability of Phase II systems to deliver both broadband data and video. Clearing the spectrum is not just a regulatory challenge. Solutions need to be developed to transfer existing services to either wireline or to new spectrum areas.

CONCLUSION

For the next 5 years or so, thanks to the vision and efforts of governments around the world, we can expect current trends in wireless communications to continue. Cellular and cellularlike services will become more global and more ubiquitous. Wireless local-loop services will provide increased competition and basic service in rural areas worldwide. Paging services will become more sophisticated, and they, too, will become even more global. Satellite services that deliver global, portable service will emerge, allowing true global roaming. Beyond these initial trends, greater allocation of spectrum will allow services for satellite system expansion, IVHS, and industrial and public safety use. After that, we will see the emergence of broadband wireless services.

That is the potential of these new telecommunications technologies. The United States has led the world with its communications and computing visions in the past, and, with mobility as part of the NII/GII agenda, it will do so again well into the next century.

Antitrust Enforcement and the Telecommunications Revolution: Friends, Not Enemies

ROBERT E. LITAN

I will start with a confession: I am a telecommunications neophyte, having only recently learned how to use the Internet. But I know from my job and from casual reading that the United States—and indeed the world—is in the midst of a telecommunications revolution that will have profound consequences for every aspect of our lives.

At the global level, telecommunications helped end the Cold War. The former communist countries could not control the flow of information that personal computers and television delivered about life in the West. Ultimately, political freedom itself spilled over from West to East.

Within the United States, telecommunications products and services are powering economic growth. According to the Council of Economic Advisers, firms engaged in the information-services sector of our economy—including computers, software, telecommunications services, and equipment—accounted for 9 percent of the nation's Gross Domestic Product in 1993. Assuming the administration's telecommunications reform proposals are enacted by the next Congress, this share could double over the following decade.

Meanwhile, advances in telecommunications have been transforming our daily lives. It is difficult to remember life without fax machines or e-mail, both of which have dramatically speeded up communications on the job. Some people may already feel the same about videoconferencing, which may be standard practice in relatively few companies now but surely will be common throughout the country in just a few short years.

In our homes, the telecommunications revolution has already dramatically lowered long-distance telephone rates, while bringing dozens of video channels to our television sets. Millions of Americans are now also using online information services and the Internet to communicate with each other, with a growing number of libraries and other databases, and with people around the world.

The future promises even more video interactivity. Once they are fully built, fiber optic highways and satellites will do for video what copper wire did for voice: allow individuals to interact with one another rather than passively receive information or entertainment.

These are not simply pie-in-the-sky predictions. By the time the Federal Communications Commission (FCC) completes its auction, investors are likely to have plunked down billions of dollars for spectrum rights that will enable providers to deliver these services to the public.

The question this paper addresses is: What public-policy issues are raised by the spread of computer- and video-based interactivity? There are many, and I certainly do not feel competent to address them all. Instead, I would like to concentrate on two very simple but powerfully important objectives that government policy makers should focus on as the telecommunications revolution proceeds.

First, policies should be in place to assure that firms in all parts of the telecommunications industry—those building the infrastructure and those developing the content that will travel over it—have the maximum incentive to innovate and to develop and deliver products and services of the highest quality at the lowest cost.

Second, the telecommunications services that are generated should be made available broadly, not just to the fortunate few. Information networks have positive externalities: the more people hooked up to the networks, the more valuable the hookups are for each participant.

Moreover, information is what economists call a public good. We educate our children, at public expense, by giving them the information and skills they will need to lead productive lives, because it is in everyone's interest for all kids to grow up to be responsible adults.

Similarly, we provide libraries, also at public expense, so that knowledge is made freely available to all segments of society.

Now that technology is revolutionizing the way information is delivered—over wires, over the air, and through computers—it is vitally important that all citizens continue to have at least some access to the information services of the modern age. This does not mean that everyone should be entitled to order movies on demand in their homes at subsidized rates. However, it does mean that great attention will have to be paid to ensuring that all of us have some basic level of access to the services and information that will be delivered over the information highways of tomorrow. By making sure that competition governs the telecommunications marketplace, the federal government can both provide incentives for innovation and encourage widespread availability of new telecommunications services.

This is an objective shared by all government agencies responsible for telecommunications policy: the FCC, the Department of Commerce, and the Antitrust Division of the Department of Justice. The rest of this paper will explain why competition is so important and how, in concrete terms, the Antitrust Division in particular has promoted and will continue to promote innovation in the telecommunications industry by protecting the competitive process.

THE IMPORTANCE OF COMPETITION

The notion that competition is critical to the development of telecommunications services has not been, and may still not be, accepted by everyone. For decades following the invention of the telephone, for example, it was widely assumed that telephone service was a natural monopoly. Public policy makers embraced this assumption by allowing AT&T to run the nation's telephone network free from competitive challenge.

More recently, some parties have suggested that the need for standards in computer-based systems is incompatible with competition. For example, Bill Gates has asserted that Microsoft's operating systems for personal computers have become industry standards and thus have characteristics of a natural monopoly. While each of these arguments in support of natural monopoly may be appealing superficially, neither, on closer examination, justifies the rejection of the central role of competition that they both imply.

Consider first the claim of natural monopoly in the telephone business. This notion was roundly rejected when the Department of Justice and Judge Harold Greene forced the breakup of AT&T in the early 1980s. The breakup was not a universally popular move, even inside the Reagan administration. In fact, according to published accounts, President Reagan, Secretary of Commerce Malcolm Baldrige, and Secretary of Defense Casper Weinberger believed that the AT&T monopoly was a national treasure that should not be broken up. But William Baxter, then the assistant attorney general for antitrust at the Justice Department and now professor emeritus at Stanford Law School, insisted that only by divesting the regional telephone monopolies from AT&T's long-distance monopoly would long-distance competitors to AT&T have a fair chance to hook up to local telephone networks.

Professor Baxter and Judge Greene were right. Look what has happened since the breakup:

- Over 100 companies have entered the long-distance telephone market, knocking AT&T's share of that business down from 100 percent to 60 percent. Real residential long-distance rates have fallen by about half, in part due to the increased competition. While the long-distance market could use even more competition—AT&T, MCI, and Sprint today account for about 90 percent of the business—the entry of so many firms rebuts the view that long-distance telephone service is a natural monopoly;
- A less well-recognized but potentially even more important product of the AT&T breakup is that it helped unleash the fiber optics revolution, making possible an exciting range of telecommunications capabilities. Corning Glass invented fiber optic cable and attempted to sell it to AT&T in the early 1970s, but AT&T was a monopolist and probably had little interest in ripping up its existing copper-wire network in order to replace it with fiber. It was not until AT&T was broken up that the use of fiber optics really took off. In part, this was because AT&T, Corning, and others working on fiber optics were by then able to bring down costs. Fiber became cheaper than the microwave technology that was once thought to be the main competitor to copper wires. However, the breakup itself almost certainly pushed things along. New entrants into the long-distance telephone business, like Sprint, MCI, and their smaller competitors, turned to Corn-

ing for fiber optic cables. Eventually, AT&T too was forced to install fiber in order to match the quality and low cost of its competitors' services.

Now that long-distance telephone markets have successfully withstood the dissolution of the natural-monopoly model, the next candidate for competition is the local telephone business. Today, this market is virtually monopolized by the regional Bell operating companies (RBOCs), which carry more than 99 percent of the local traffic in their regions. The local market may look very different in the near future, however.

It is possible, if not likely, that within a few years the coaxial cable owned by cable television operators will be delivering local telephone traffic, just as it is doing today for nearly 400,000 customers in the United Kingdom. In addition, a variety of wireless technologies—including cellular, specialized mobile radio, and the new personal communications services portions of the spectrum—could create powerful competition to land-line telephone services.

Of course, cable and other alternatives to the RBOCs' local telephone monopolies will arrive only if state and local regulators permit them to compete. So far, only a few states have taken steps to remove restrictions to entry into the telephone business. Later, this paper will address the need for other states to eliminate these artificial and unnecessary barriers to entry.

What about the claim that the need for standards leaves little room for competition? This argument is flat wrong. It may well be true that once a standard has been accepted in the marketplace, such as the QWERTY layout on a typewriter, competition is no longer possible. But, with the one qualification I will discuss shortly, competition should actually govern the development of the standards themselves.

Microsoft proves this point. Microsoft gained a monopoly in operating systems for personal computers in the 1980s by successfully marketing DOS and Windows, which became industry standards. There was nothing unlawful about this. But then the company adopted certain licensing practices—"per processor" licenses that taxed competing operating systems and set lengthy terms and large minimum commitments. This effectively froze competing operating systems out of the original equipment market, the largest channel for distributing this type of software. The Justice Department sued Microsoft because these practices, coupled with restrictive nondisclosure agreements imposed on developers of applications software, unlawfully entrenched the company's monopoly and thereby deprived competitors of a fair shot at becoming the next standard. Microsoft has signed a consent decree, which the District Court for the District of Columbia disapproved in February 1995 but which I fully expect the Court of Appeals to approve on appeal. When it does, this decree will help level the playing field in the PC operating systems market.

The Microsoft case teaches an important lesson. It is perfectly legitimate to own a technology or product that becomes a standard, but it is against the law to erect barricades to competing, would-be standards. This proposition is especially important in high-technology industries, where rapid innovation may create frequent opportunities for new standards to replace old ones. If the owners of the old standards are allowed to use any means to block entry of the new, then innovation itself will be discouraged and consumers will lose out.

The one qualification to the proposition that competition should govern the development of standards is that in some cases, it may be in society's interest for competitors to agree on standards, or, in effect, to work jointly to create standards. For example, manufacturers may lawfully cooperate to set quality standards, saving regulators the time and expense of certification. A number of bodies in the telecommunications and computer fields perform similar functions.

But even in these cases, the joint-venture partners in the standards process must not abuse their legitimate collaboration to distort the competitive process. Thus, standards-setting bodies should be open to all parties who meet reasonable criteria for membership. In addition, the standards-setting process must be a fair one and not serve simply as a device for preventing new competitors or new standards from entering the market.

In sum, competition must remain the central governing principle for the information age. Competition encourages continued innovation and guarantees consumers the lowest prices for telecommunications and information services, and by so doing it promotes the widespread availability of these services.

If there is any doubt about these propositions, one need only look to Europe and Japan. Both regions have continued to follow the state-directed, monopoly model in telecommunications, and they now find themselves playing catch-up to the United States. For instance, it was recently reported that Japan's telephone monopoly, NTT, is far behind the U.S. regional telephone companies in laying fiber optic cable (Hamilton, 1994). In addition, European governments have been taken to task for sheltering their telecommunications giants from both domestic and foreign competition (*The Economist*, 1994). This criticism is not hard to understand. One recent study projects that an end to telephone monopolies in Europe would not only lower prices but improve quality by 40 percent (Hudson, 1994).

The benefits of competition are being recognized closer to home. In September, Canadian regulators took a major step to promote competition by allowing telephone companies to transmit video images and by opening up local telephone markets to competition from cable television operators and other sources. If the United States wants to continue to lead the world in telecommunications innovation, it must act soon to move in a direction similar to Canada's; that is, it must clear away the remaining obstacles to fair and effective competition throughout the telecommunications industry.

PRESERVING AND PROMOTING COMPETITION THROUGH ANTITRUST ENFORCEMENT

Along with the Federal Trade Commission (FTC), the Justice Department's Antitrust Division is charged by federal law with protecting and promoting competition. Next, this paper will consider how the division has been fulfilling this mandate in ways that affect the future of telecommunications.

Merger Enforcement

One of the defining characteristics of the current revolution in the telecommunications field is the dizzying pace of corporate mergers. It seems that not a week goes by without one or two major mergers or corporate alliances being announced, each advertised as an ideal way to accelerate the building of the information superhighway by combining the unique talents and expertise of the two partners.

In many cases, this may be true, and the division will not stand in the way of these arrangements. However, we draw the line, as the law requires us to, at mergers that threaten to concentrate economic power in particular markets or to erect barriers to the entry of competitors.

Mergers involving telecommunications and computer firms can pose special problems for those who enforce antitrust laws, because many of the firms in these industries already have dominant, or even monopoly, positions. The seven RBOCs, for example, each currently has a monopoly in local telephone service. The same is true for almost all cable television firms in the markets they serve. Other high-technology firms also have substantial market power in various lines of business.

Firms that are already dominant in their markets surely know that neither the division nor the FTC is likely to permit them to engage in horizontal acquisitions, that is, purchases of direct competitors. As a result, many of the high-technology mergers we have seen so far involve the marriages of firms dominant in one market with firms in related markets—such as RBOCs proposing mergers with cable companies, telephone companies active in different geographic areas proposing mergers, and so on. The critical question posed by these mergers is whether they will allow one or both of the firms with dominance in one market to extend market power to a second market—a special danger where the acquiring firm is a regulated monopoly. If so, antitrust enforcers try to persuade the parties to revise their plans in ways that remove the anticompetitive effects of the transaction. If this fails, we will sue to halt the merger.

Two recent examples demonstrate how it is possible to prune the anticompetitive effects from otherwise lawful telecommunications mergers. The first is the union between AT&T and McCaw Cellular Communication, both dominant players in their respective markets. As noted earlier, AT&T still has about 60 percent of the long-distance telephone market. Overall, McCaw carries about 30 percent of the nation's cellular traffic, but in some regions of the country this figure is closer to 50 percent. In seeking to acquire McCaw, AT&T clearly wanted to provide seamless local and long-distance cellular service to customers.

Without any conditions, however, this proposed merger posed risks to competition in several markets. Under the original proposal, the parties wanted to be able to market to their customers a combined long-distance/local-service cellular package, without giving them a choice of another long-distance carrier. Given McCaw's market power in various localities and AT&T's market power in long-distance, this proposal could have significantly distorted competition in the long-distance market by diverting customers away from other long-distance companies based on factors other than quality or price, further entrenching AT&T's already dominant position in long distance.

To address this problem, the division conditioned its approval of the merger on McCaw's providing to competing long-distance carriers equal access to its subscribers. This is what the RBOCs now are required to do for long-distance traffic on their land lines, and the Department of Justice has proposed that they do the same if they are allowed to provide long-distance service to cellular customers. In addition, the consent decree that the parties signed prohibits AT&T from offering its local and long-distance cellular services as a bundle; the company must instead separately price each service.

The AT&T/McCaw merger also posed a threat to competition in local cellular markets. AT&T currently is the dominant manufacturer of equipment for cellular carriers, including many of the RBOCs that compete with McCaw. Given the nature of cellular systems, once a carrier begins purchasing a particular brand of equipment, it gets locked in to that brand for some period of time. The additional danger posed by the merger was that AT&T could exploit its position in the cellular-equipment market by raising prices or denying or delaying the delivery of parts and other services to RBOCs that compete with McCaw in local cellular service. Knowing this, rival cellular carriers and AT&T/McCaw could implicitly decide to keep cellular prices high. The consent decree prevents this result by prohibiting AT&T from such conduct. In addition, it addresses the lock-in problem by allowing, under certain circumstances, cellular equipment customers of AT&T to sell back their equipment to AT&T, if they want to, at cost minus a reasonable allowance for depreciation.

The second telecommunications merger approved subject to important conditions is the purchase by British Telecommunications (BT) of a 20 percent interest in MCI, as well as the creation of a global joint venture between the two companies. This transaction raised important telecommunications issues in an international context. Like AT&T and McCaw, MCI wanted its equity partnership with BT in order to enhance its ability to offer seamless telecommunications services, in this case on a worldwide basis. If BT did not have market power in telecommunications services in the United Kingdom, it is unlikely that either the proposed equity investment by BT in MCI or the joint venture would pose any competitive risks.

But BT was and remains the dominant telephone company in the United Kingdom. By virtue of this dominance, BT would gain from the proposed transaction both the incentives and the ability to favor its joint venture with MCI in pricing, interconnection, and possibly other ways—all to the detriment of U.S. users of other global telecommunications providers. If this occurred, then the prices on telephone traffic between our two countries would increase.

Accordingly, the division imposed several conditions on the BT/MCI transaction. Most important, the parties agreed to publish detailed information about the terms and conditions of services that BT provides to the joint venture and to MCI. This information will give ammunition to any disfavored competitors that wish to lodge complaints with regulatory authorities in either the United States or the United Kingdom. Such a "transparency" provision is less intrusive and less costly, but no less effective, than direct regulation.

In addition, the consent decree prohibits BT from providing to either the joint venture or to MCI confidential information about other international telecommunications providers. Moreover, the parties agreed that if a significant act of discrimination in favor of the joint venture or MCI occurs in the future, the department may seek modification of the decree to strengthen its nondiscrimination provisions.

What about future mergers in the telecommunications industry? It is difficult to be specific, because some are pending now before the division. It is possible, however, to offer several broad comments on the relation between competition policy and mergers in the industry.

There has been much talk about "the" information superhighway. In fact, several highways appear to be in the works—land-line telephone, land-line cable, and various wireless technologies—all competing to deliver voice and video content to businesses and homes around the country. No one really knows which of these highways will be successful. That is what markets are for—to let the firms that are now spending billions of dollars to build these highways fight it out.

For those charged with enforcing the antitrust laws, three concerns are paramount.

First, we do not want any highway owner that now has a regulated monopoly in its market to cross-subsidize. That is, cable operators who want to enter telephone markets, or local telephone companies that may eventually gain entry into long-distance markets, should fund their expansion only from the capital markets and not from their customers. The same is true for regulated telephone companies hoping to offer video and other services. To allow any other result is to permit the marketplace to favor monopolists, to the detriment of consumers.

Second, at least for the next several years, we should not allow the owner of any one highway in a given geographic area to merge with or buy out a competing highway. If, for example, local telephone companies were permitted to merge with their cable television competitors in the same service territory, neither firm would retain the incentive to develop and supply the new interactive services that consumers have been promised. This situation may change once technology affords consumers more ways to receive information in the home. In the meantime, however, it is prudent to prohibit for a reasonable period marriages of cable and telephone firms operating in the same service areas; the administration has suggested 5 years.

Third, we will be especially watchful of mergers or joint ventures between owners of highways and owners of content. Such transactions may create strong incentives for the integrated entity to deny competing programmers access to the highways. In such cases, we will be prepared either to block the merger or to condition it on "equal access" requirements that prevent such discrimination, as we did with TCI's acquisition of Liberty Media.

Removing Barriers To Entry

It is one thing to prevent mergers that threaten to choke off competition. It is another to ensure that such competition is allowed to take place. Current law, however, largely presumes that certain telecommunications markets should be monopolies and therefore insulated from competition. Therefore, unless the Supreme Court holds that federal law is unconstitutional (as have three federal courts), local telephone companies will remain barred from offering video services in their service territories. As noted earlier, local telephone companies are legally insulated from competition in all but a few states. In addition, the consent decree governing the AT&T breakup prohibits the RBOCs from competing in long-distance telephone services.

In 1994, Congress came very close to enacting comprehensive legislation that would have paved the way for erasing each of these barriers to competition. The Clinton administration worked closely with Congress to achieve passage of this legislation and intends to continue that partnership in 1995. In the meantime, the administration urges the states to remove barriers preventing new entrants in the local telephone business. New York, Wisconsin, Illinois, and a number of other states have already taken such steps or will soon do so.

Competition is vital if America is to maintain its leadership in telecommunications technologies and services. Competition also will best advance the goal of universal service, since competition will encourage providers to lower their own costs, and thus their prices to consumers.

Still, even a vibrantly competitive telecommunications marketplace will not deliver its services to all consumers. Some will lack the income to buy. Others services may be too costly for private suppliers profitably to provide. The most efficient and least distorting way to fill these gaps is to provide subsidies to those who would otherwise not be able to purchase competitively priced telecommunications services. The legislation considered by Congress last year would have directed the appropriate federal and state regulatory bodies to move in this direction.

CONCLUSION

The message here has been a simple one. Monopolies in telecommunications are dead or dying. This is good news, for only through vigorous competition will the telecommunications revolution we are now witnessing bring its full benefits to American consumers. The Justice Department's Antitrust Division is working hard to make this happen. We hope that Congress will assist us in this task by enacting soon the comprehensive telecommunications legislation that is so sorely needed.

REFERENCES

Hamilton, D.P. *Wall Street Journal.* August 15, 1994. Getting wired: big fiber-optic project is private sector's job, Japan reformers say. A1.

Hudson, R.L. *Wall Street Journal.* September 30, 1994. World business (A special report): An industrial revolution. R20.

The Economist. August 13, 1994. Europe's dash for the future. 13.

Contributors

STEVEN D. DORFMAN is a senior vice president and member of the Office of the Chairman of GM Hughes Electronics Corp. and its subsidiary, Hughes Aircraft Company, and president of the Hughes Telecommunications and Space Company. He joined Hughes in 1957 and, in subsequent years, held positions of increasing responsibility in management, systems engineering, and electro-optics. Mr. Dorfman was named to his present position in October 1993 after serving more than 2 years as president of Hughes Space and Communications Company. Prior to Mr. Dorfman's Space and Communications Company assignment, he was president and chief executive officer of Hughes Communications Inc. (HCI), the Hughes subsidiary that owns and operates communications satellites. Mr. Dorfman was elected to the National Academy of Engineering in 1992. He received his bachelor's degree in electrical engineering from the University of Florida and his master's degree in the same field from the University of Southern California.

ROBERT E. KAHN has been president of the Corporation for National Research Initiatives (CNRI) in Reston, Virginia since 1986. CNRI was created as a not-for-profit organization to provide leadership and funding for research and development of the national information infrastructure. From 1972 to 1985, he was a program manager, deputy director, and ultimately director of the Information Processing Techniques Office at the Defense Advanced Research Projects Agency. He is a member of the National Academy of Engineering, a fellow of the Institute of Electrical and Electronic Engineers, and twice recipient of the Secretary of Defense Meritorious Civilian Service Award. Dr. Kahn received his B.E.E. from City College of New York and his M.A. and Ph.D. degrees in electrical engineering from Princeton University.

ROBERT E. LITAN is an associate director of the Office of Management and Budget. At the time this paper was written, Dr. Litan was deputy assistant attorney general in the Antitrust Division of the U.S. Justice Department, where he supervised the division's civil non-merger enforcement program and the development of the division's policies affecting regulated industries. He came to this position in September 1993, following 9 years as a senior fellow at the Brookings Institution, where he also was director of two research centers in the institution's Economics Studies Program. Dr. Litan formerly was a partner and then counsel to Powell, Goldstein, Frazer & Murphy, an associate at Arnold & Porter, and the regulatory and energy specialist for President Carter's Council of Economic Advisers. He has a B.S. in economics from the Wharton School of Finance, a J.D. from Yale Law School, and a Ph.D. in economics from Yale University.

JOHN E. MAJOR is the senior vice president and assistant chief corporate staff officer for Motorola. In those roles, he oversees Motorola's product, software, and manufacturing research, as well as manages Motorola's global telecommunications network. One of his key initiatives is leading Motorola's effort to be a global leader in software technology. Previously, he managed the Worldwide Systems Group that developed and manufactured private voice and data radio systems for public-safety and business users. Mr. Major serves on the boards of directors of the Telecommunications Industry Association and the Electronics Industry Association. He is a member of the National Academy of Sciences, where he serves on the Computer Science and Telecommunications Board. His degrees include a B.S. in mechanical and aerospace engineering from the University of Rochester, an M.S. in mechanical engineering from the University of

Illinois, an M.B.A. from Northwestern University, and a J.D. from Loyola University.

JOHN S. MAYO is president emeritus of AT&T Bell Laboratories. He served as president from July 1991 until March 1995. Throughout his career at Bell Laboratories, Dr. Mayo has played an important role in the development of digital technologies that have brought the world to the threshold of the information age. Dr. Mayo is a fellow of the Institute of Electrical and Electronic Engineers (IEEE). Among his awards is the 1990 National Medal of Technology, given for his contributions to the technological foundations for information age communications. Dr. Mayo was elected to the National Academy of Engineering in 1979. He received his B.S., M.S., and Ph.D. degrees in electrical engineering from North Carolina State University in 1952, 1953, and 1955, respectively.

ROBERT W. STEARNS is vice president of corporate development for the Compaq Computer Corp. He directs the company's strategic planning and business development activities, including acquisitions, joint ventures and alliances, advanced market research, and technology assessment. He is also responsible for coordinating legislative policy issues and Compaq's involvement in various technical standards-setting organizations and trade associations. Mr. Stearns joined Compaq in July 1993 from McKinsey & Co., where he served as a consultant to high-technology clients. He previously held senior management positions at a number of technology companies, including Motorola/Codex, Banyan Systems, Motorola's Information Systems Group, and Management Technologies Inc., a decision-support software company that he founded. Mr. Stearns speaks and writes frequently on matters related to the computer and telecommunications industries and innovation in technological organizations. He graduated with a B.S. degree in chemistry from Brown University in 1971 and an M.S. degree from the Massachusetts Institute of Technology in 1973.